When, What and How

In each CSA exam, a physical examinat[ion is required in] approximately one third of cases. General pr[actitioners] are time pressured and clinical examination[s need to be performed] efficiently and effectively in the CSA, and as a General Practitioner, you need to be skilled at choosing when, what and how to examine, and be proficient in performing examination routines. Both your choice of examination and examination technique will be marked.

When
Indications for clinical examination in General Practice

- To investigate clinical possibilities suggested by history taking
- To address patient concerns
- To monitor long term conditions
- To initiate or monitor medication
- To assess severity of a condition
- To exclude important red flags (e.g. photophobia in meningitis)

What
Choosing appropriate examination components

Your examination choice should be limited to examining for signs that will influence or aid your management, including the management of patient concerns. At first you may be inclined to examine more frequently or broadly to address your own concerns and uncertainty. This is no bad thing, as thoroughness can contribute to proficiency and aid familiarity with the range of normal. The videos and guides included in this book will help you select and perform focused examinations.

As a rule of thumb, the practitioner that 'under examines' is of more concern than one that 'over examines'. Whilst he/she may be slower, they are less likely to miss important clinical signs than one who does not examine. As you become more experienced, your ability to select relevant and focused examination components will improve.

The presence of red flag alarm features in the history, or during examination, should prompt a more detailed examination routine. For example, a man presents with back pain. He requires a back examination. There are no red flags in the history or on examination, therefore a brief and focused examination is adequate. Should the patient for instance have a history of leg weakness, or weakness is discovered during the examination, the doctor should proceed to a more detailed neurological examination.

If you are unsure in the CSA, and in real life, it is safer to over examine than under examine. The cost to you in the exam is that you will have less time to manage the case and may lose marks in the clinical management domain.

How
How will you approach the examination?

The acronym **SETUP** can help you think through the steps.

Site
Where is it most appropriate to examine with the patient?
Sitting in a chair, standing, or on the examination couch?

Exposure
Do you need the patient to remove any clothing?

Timing
How much time should you allow?
Most examinations in the CSA should take no more than 2 minutes.

Utensils
What equipment should you use?

Protection
How will you protect yourself and your patient during the examination?
Think about patient dignity and the use of chaperones.

Contents

Section 1: An overview of physical examination in the CSA

When, what and how 5
Chaperones and patient care 7
Proficient examination 9
Three examination scenarios...9
How examinations in the CSA differ 11
The evidence base 12
How to use this guide 13
Examination videos...14

Section 2: The specifics of physical examination in the CSA

Head 15
Headache 16
Red eye 19
Benign paroxysmal positional vertigo..22
Visual impairment...23
Cranial nerves 26

Neck...34
Thyroid swelling 35
Neck lumps 37

Chest..39
Breathlessness of unknown aetiology 40
Asthma exacerbation 43
Chest Infection / COPD exacerbation 45

Palpitations 47
Hypertension 49

Arm...52
Shoulder 53
Arm neurological 57
Elbow 62
Hand 64

Abdomen..68
Abdominal pain 69
Rectal bleeding 72
Low back pain 73

Pelvis 76
Vaginal discharge 77
Pelvic pain 79
Intermenstrual bleeding 81
Male genital 84

Leg 86
Hip pain 87
Knee pain 90
Leg neurological 94
Painful foot 96
Peripheral vascular disease and diabetic foot 98

Copyright 2019 Nicholas Boeckx. John Marlow

All rights reserved. No part of this publication may be reproduced, stored in a retrieval system, or transmitted, in any form or by any means except as permitted by the UK Copyright, Designs and Patents Act 1988, without the prior permission of the authors.

First published 3 Oct. 2019

ISBN-10: 1729061567
ISBN-13: 978-1729061565

Foreword

The aim of this book is to help trainees and trainers prepare for the Royal College of General Practitioners' (RCGP) Clinical Skills Assessment (CSA). The guidance and walkthrough videos will help you to gain a better understanding of the approach to physical examination necessary to meet the examination standard.

In the CSA, candidates are required to select and perform the physical examination expected of a competent general practitioner within the context of a 10-minute general practice consultation. Translating that standard into practical guidance for an individual case is complex, not least due to the differences in approach that exist amongst trainees, trainers and examiners. This book provides practical guidance by summarising the consensus opinion of 293 GP trainers and 16 CSA examiners for a series of typical CSA scenarios. The findings are presented along with notes and guidance.

Dr Boeckx and Dr Marlow are experienced CSA tutors and Fellows of the RCGP and have taught on the CSA since its inception. Both teach regularly for the RCGP on physical examination alongside senior examiners. Their work has been recognised by the RCGP with a Quality Award. If you are preparing for the CSA or helping others prepare, this book is here to help you.

Chaperones and Patient Care

The GMC provides clear guidance on physical examination which you should be familiar with and apply in the CSA and in your practice. It is summarised here:

Before conducting an intimate examination, you should:
a) Explain to the patient why an examination is necessary and give them the opportunity to ask questions.

b) Explain what the examination will entail, in a way the patient understands, so that they have a clear idea what to expect, including any pain or discomfort.

c) Obtain the patient's permission before the examination and record this.

d) Offer the patient a chaperone. This applies whether or not you are the same gender as the patient.

e) If dealing with a child or young person you must assess their capacity to consent to the examination and if they lack the capacity to consent, you should seek their parent's consent.

f) Give the patient privacy to undress and dress, and keep them covered as much as possible to maintain their dignity; do not help the patient to remove clothing unless they have asked you to, or you have checked with them that they want you to help.

During the examination, you should:
a) Explain what you are going to do before you do it and, if this differs from what you have told the patient before, explain why and seek the patient's permission.

b) Stop the examination if the patient asks you to.

c) Keep discussion relevant and don't make unnecessary personal comments.

Use of Chaperones

a) A chaperone should usually be a health professional who has had relevant training, and you must be satisfied that the chaperone will:
- be sensitive and respect the patient's dignity and confidentiality.
- reassure the patient if they show signs of distress or discomfort.
- be familiar with the procedures involved in a routine intimate examination.
- stay for the whole examination and be able to see what the doctor is doing, if practical.
- be prepared to raise concerns if they are concerned about the doctor's behaviour or actions.

b) A relative or friend of the patient is not an acceptable chaperone.

c) If either you or the patient does not want the examination to go ahead without a chaperone present, you may offer to defer the examination to a later date when a suitable chaperone will be available, as long as the delay would not adversely affect the patient's health.

d) If you do not want to examine without a chaperone present, but the patient has declined having one, you must explain clearly why you want a chaperone present. Ultimately the patient's clinical needs must take precedence. You may wish to consider referring the patient to a colleague who would be willing to examine them without a chaperone provided a delay would not adversely affect the patient's health.

e) You should record any discussion about chaperones and the outcome in the patient's medical record. If a chaperone is present, you should record that fact and make a note of their identity. If the patient does not want a chaperone, you should record that an offer was made and declined.
General Medical Council (2013) Good medical practice London, and (2012) Protecting children and young people: the responsibilities of all doctors London.

Trainees often ask how they should raise the need for a chaperone. A typical example would be: 'For this kind of examination, it is normal to have a Chaperone. Is that okay?'

A pause afterwards allows the patient to consent, or initiate further discussion, and helps ensure the consultation is shared. Shared consulting contributes to your interpersonal skills mark.

Proficient Examination

Your technical proficiency in physical examination is assessed and contributes to your mark for data gathering.

Professional physical examinations have several attributes.

- Respect for patient safety, comfort and dignity is prioritised.

- Clear directions are given to the patient.

- Routines are slick and automatic (a practised and fluid examination moving from one aspect to the next without the need to think through individual steps).

- Examination inspires patient confidence (see the above point).

- The examination steps are based on best evidence and practice.

Three Examination Scenarios

There are three potential scenarios which arise in a CSA case.

Scenario 1: An examination is not indicated (not all cases require examination).

Scenario 2: An examination is indicated but you are not required to perform the examination.

Scenario 3: An examination is indicated which you are required to perform.

If this is a scenario 2 case, you will be given information of the examination findings. This could be by verbal instruction from the examiner, by written or photographic information, or by the examination findings being displayed on your iPad- scroll down to view these where applicable.

There is a temptation to read the information given and restart the consultation immediately thereafter, but are you ready to restart? When you regain eye contact, you need to be ready to summarise the findings to the patient and outline the management options. Be mindful that you are in a situation that does not reflect everyday practice. You have lost the time that is naturally available during examination, or while washing your hands after, in which you would normally interpret and process the findings.

Examiners and role players recognise the situation is alien and will allow you a brief period to read and process the information on the card. The consultation will resume when you regain eye contact with the patient and start speaking. Take time to read and interpret the examination findings on the card, in relation to the history. Resist the pressure to restart the consultation before you are ready, as doing so can negatively impact on your conclusions and subsequent management plan.

Have You Got the Full Picture?
Note that the findings you receive depends on what you have asked for. If you don't ask for an important aspect of the examination, you won't receive information about it. Take care to request reasonable and relevant examinations and tests available in general practice. What is a reasonable and relevant examination or test? The answer is any examination or test readily available in general practice, for example fundoscopy, urinalysis or peak flow testing.

Making a premature judgement on the diagnosis is a common cause of error known as confirmation bias. To avoid the trap, search for additional information that may refute or support your working diagnosis. Are there further examinations or tests that might alter your conclusion? A classic example of confirmation bias is the failure to consider pregnancy in a woman of childbearing age with abdominal pain.

Examination findings are given on a card or verbally and may also be displayed on the computer screen. You will be given time to read and absorb the findings before the role player asks any questions.

Remember, if no information appears on the computer screen and you have not been given instructions or handed a card by the examiner this means you are required to examine. Get up and examine as you would normally do in your practice. Do not sit and stare at the examiner hoping for a card to be handed over!

How Examinations in the CSA Differ

Whilst the CSA tries to replicate a normal surgery as best it can, there are some differences between examining a patient in the CSA and examining a patient back in the surgery.

The first notable difference is that prior to commencing examination you are expected to outline in full the examination components you would like to complete using lay terminology.

For example, in an asthma exacerbation case you may inform the role player; 'Now you've told me what has been going on, I would like to listen to your chest, ask you to do a blowing test, check your pulse rate and pop a device on your finger to measure your oxygen levels. Is that okay?'.

You might not be used to doing this, but it is good practice for everyday consulting. It helps the consultation be patient centred, by signposting what is about to happen. It is also something the GMC stipulates before performing an intimate examination. I suggest you integrate it into your everyday routine. If you forget to do so, the role-player is instructed to prompt you by asking, 'What would you like to examine?'

Intimate Examinations

The second way in which physical examination in the CSA differs from normal surgery is that certain examinations are less likely to be performed. You will not be expected to perform intimate examinations, although may be offered a model to examine. You will still need to explain your intended examination to the patient. How to do this is covered later in this book. Remember to request a chaperone to be present.

The Evidence Base

This evidence base for this book is a survey by Dr Boeckx of 293 GP trainers and 16 CSA examiners which has been analysed to provide guidance about physical examination of common General Practice cases. Excerpts from the original data set are displayed alongside the relevant topics.

The physical examinations suggested in this book are informed by the consensus opinion in the survey, and the expert advice of senior CSA examiners on how to interpret and use the data collected to best provide guidance to candidates. It is appropriate here to express thanks to Robin Simpson and the RCGP West Midlands CSA course team.

The CSA Case Writing Process

During the case writing process, it is the role of the focus group of CSA examiners to reach a consensus opinion to the question, 'In this specific scenario what would a safe GP in a competent 10-minute consultation be expected to examine?' As previously stated, the evidence base behind the guidance provided in this book was collected through a survey. The survey was constructed in such a way as to replicate the case writing process. It presented typical CSA scenarios to the survey group, which functioned as our 'focus group'. The responses from the CSA examiners and trainers were analysed separately giving a consensus opinion from each. Our groups replicated the CSA case calibration process, albeit at a larger scale than in the CSA focus group process.

By replicating the processes used in the CSA case construction and being open to the same limitations and bias, the methodology provides a valid representation of the standards expected in the CSA examination. Separate data collection for trainers and CSA examiners allows the standards expected by the two groups to be compared, the overall difference of which was reassuringly small.

How to Use this Guide

For the same clinical topic what you choose to examine should vary depending on the details of the case. For example, a presentation of headache may prompt you to examine blood pressure, visual acuity and fundoscopy. The presence of additional information, for example that the patient is dizzy or is worried about acoustic neuroma, should prompt you to perform additional examinations.

To help your selection we have provided a list of relevant examinations for each clinical topic. Choose the most appropriate from the list dependent on the details of the case. To simplify your task of choosing what to examine the choices have been divided into:

Commonly required examination components
and
Additional examination components

You are likely to be expected to examine the common components in each case. Examine an additional component if the specified indication is present. Don't neglect the additional examination components. The CSA exam lends itself towards testing your ability to appropriately select and examine additional components that support or refute your diagnosis.

For each examination, the guidance focuses on WHAT to include and HOW to move through the examination efficiently and fluidly.

To keep the guidance concise, it is assumed that you will be able to perform the basic elements of each examination. Tips are provided regarding common errors of examination technique, and on how to perform more complex aspects of examination.

The guidance in the following chapters is organised by anatomical region, starting with the head and working down the body. Within each region the more commonly required examinations are listed first.

Examination Videos

You can access online walkthrough examination videos by using the embedded QR codes. Online you will find a list of resources, including videos, that demonstrate how to perform the different examinations, special manoeuvres and tests described in this book. To access the main menu, use the QR code link shown here.

Head

Headache 16
Red Eye 19
Benign Paroxysmal Positional Vertigo 22
Visual Impairment 23
Cranial Nerves 26

- Bell's Palsy
- Acoustic neuroma
- Tunnel vision
- Visual field defects
- Trigeminal Neuralgia
- Raised Intracranial Pressure
- Facial Herpes Zoster
- Facial Stroke
- Myasthenia Gravis

Headache

Common Components

Inspection
Inspection findings will not be replicated by CSA role players. If signs are present an examination findings card will be given. Look for evidence of rashes (meningitis), red eye (glaucoma) or systemic illness (infection).

Blood pressure
Blood pressure recording is often expected by patients but is an uncommon cause of headache. Measuring blood pressure in a patient concerned about hypertension as a cause for headache will help demonstrate a patient centred approach, gaining marks under the interpersonal skills domain. A normal blood pressure reading in this scenario provides evidence to make reassurance effective.

Fundoscopy
Look for the presence of papilloedema.

Additional Components

Visual disturbance in the history
(except aura typical of migraine)
Check visual acuity, visual fields, pupil reactivity & fundoscopy (for corneal, optic nerve, and macula pathology)

New onset headaches in patients aged over 50
Palpate the temporal artery (temporal arteritis risk).

Features of raised intracranial pressure
Examine CN 6, and perform fundoscopy for papilloedema.

Risk factors for neck problems such as spondylosis or a history of tension headache
Check for neck muscle tenderness and stiffness.

Vertigo
Examine CN 5,7,8,9 and perform otoscopy.

Headache

Examination Clues

- **Migraine**

No neurological signs are expected on examination in between attacks, so if abnormalities are present, consider an alternative diagnosis. First presentation typically occurs below the age of 30 (80% of cases). New onset migraine symptoms in the over 50's should prompt greater scrutiny for sinister pathology.

- **Temporal Arteritis**

Loss of temporal artery pulsation and scalp tenderness are features typical of temporal arteritis. Cases are most common between the ages of 60-80.

- **Raised intracranial pressure**

Raised intracranial pressure is suggested by papilloedema (blurred disc margins, on a swollen and elevated optic disc with loss of venous pulsation and flame shaped haemorrhages), third nerve palsy (dilated pupil, with the eye looking down and out) or sixth nerve palsy (loss of lateral gaze). Expect a history suggesting an underlying cause e.g. intracranial bleeding, tumour, hydrocephalus.

Case Example

Case

A 26-year-old female presents with headache consistent with classical migraine. There are no alarming features in the history or on examination. Choose the examinations you would expect from a safe GP in a competent 10-minute consultation.

Discussion

Results from the survey indicate that blood pressure and fundoscopy are common components expected by most examiners and trainers. The need to perform neck movements and a cranial nerve assessment are less commonly expected.

We suggest you allow your examination to be guided by the absence or presence of the indications for examination as explained in this guide along with the base rate probability of the conditions.

Consensus opinion

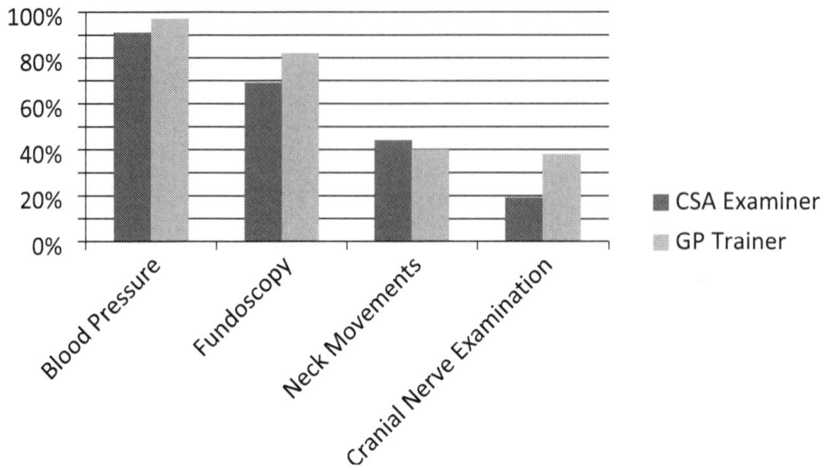
100%
80%
60%
40%
20%
0%
Blood Pressure
Fundoscopy
Neck Movements
Cranial Nerve Examination
CSA Examiner
GP Trainer

Red Eye

Common Components

Inspection
Inspection findings will not be replicated by CSA role players. If signs are present an examination findings card will be given. The examination card may reveal evidence of abnormalities affecting the eyelids, conjunctiva or iris.

Additional Components

Foreign body / Contact Lens Use
Perform fundoscopy and stain the eye with fluorescein to detect evidence of corneal injury.

Reduced visual acuity
Test the visual fields, pupil reactivity & fundoscopy (for corneal, optic nerve or macula pathology).

Examination Clues

- **Conjunctivitis**

Mild conjunctival injection (conjunctival redness with a broad distribution - see diagram), discharge, often bilateral.

- **Acute angle closure glaucoma**

Decreased visual acuity, hazy cornea, semi dilated or oval pupil. The pain of acute glaucoma is <u>severe</u> and often associated with vomiting. Patients usually present age >50.

- **Keratitis**

Corneal defects on fluorescein staining. Visual acuity is affected in some but not all. A foreign body sensation and photophobia is common. Contact lens use is a risk factor.

Red Eye

- **Anterior uveitis**

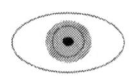

Redness localising to the edge of the iris (ciliary injection- see diagram), constricted or irregular pupils, reduced visual acuity, pain on accommodation.

- **Corneal Abrasion**

Staining with fluorescein. Localised redness may occur.

- **Endophthalmitis**

Hypopyon (a white collection in the anterior chamber), chemosis (oedema of the conjunctiva), marked pain.

- **Scleritis**

A localised patch of redness, typically in patients >50 years of age and associated with severe pain (as opposed to usually painless episcleritis).

Case Example

Case Details

A 51-year-old male presents with an irritated red eye. The cause is bacterial conjunctivitis. There are no alarming features in the history. There are no alarming findings on examination. Choose the examinations you would expect from a safe GP in a competent 10-minute consultation.

Discussion

Inspection is the common component expected by examiners in the presentation of a red eye. The examination findings will be presented on an examinations card which may include a picture of the conjunctiva and or fundus. There are a wide variety of causes which can be helpfully divided by the distribution of redness and the presence of pain. The following are consistent with an acutely painful red eye; acute angle closure glaucoma, keratitis, acute anterior uveitis, foreign body, corneal abrasion, scleritis and endophthalmitis. An acutely painless red eye may be due to; conjunctivitis, episcleritis, and subconjunctival haemorrhage.

Red Eye

The need to perform other components are less which are less commonly expected should be guided by the case details.

Consensus opinion

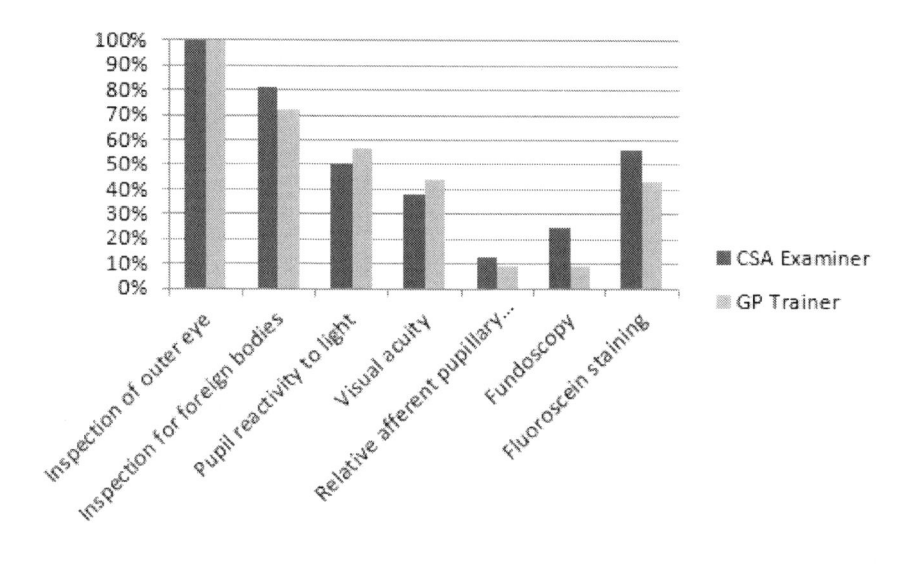

Benign Paroxysmal Positional Vertigo

Common Components

Dix-Hallpike Manoeuvre (Test for BPPV)
Warn the patient that they may experience dizziness. With the couch flat, position the patient so that when they lie flat their shoulders will be level with the end of the couch.

With the patient sitting rotate the head by 45 to the left (to test the left ear).

Whilst supporting the patient's head lie the patient down quickly with their head extended to 30 degrees below the level of the couch.

Observe for nystagmus (a positive test). If negative, consider repeating with the head turned to the other side.

NB: It is important to support the patient when they return to a sitting position as this may precipitate further vertigo.

Treatment (Epley Manoeuvre)
The initial head rotation should be made towards the affected side.

Start the same as for the Dix-Hallpike manoeuvre but hold the position for 30 seconds. Then rotate the head by 90 degrees to the opposite side, ask the patient to roll on their side so they are facing the floor, then sit up with their head in the same position looking over their shoulder and finally ask them to bring their chin to their chest. Hold each position for 30 seconds. Remember to support the patient when they return to a sitting position as this may precipitate further vertigo.

Visual Impairment

Common Components

Inspection
The listed signs here are not replicated by CSA role players. If signs are present an examination findings card will be given. Inspect the eyelids, conjunctiva, pupil size, and look for a foreign body.

Visual Acuity
Test visual acuity using a Snellen chart (present in every CSA exam room).

Visual Fields
Test visual fields by confrontation.

Pupil Reactivity to Light
Test pupil reactivity to light for corneal, optic nerve, & macula pathology.

Additional Components

Foreign body
Fundoscopy with fluorescein staining for corneal disruption.

Visual Field Defect confirmed on examination
Test Cranial Nerves 2,3,4,6.

Diplopia
Test Cranial nerves 2,3,4,6.

Examination Clues

- **Central Visual Defects**
  Consider: Age related macular degeneration
              Optic neuropathy
              Retinal artery occlusion

Visual Impairment

- **Peripheral Visual Defects**

Consider: Glaucoma
Retinal detachment
Branch retinal artery occlusion
Retinitis pigmentosa

- **Central Retinal Vein Occlusion**

CRVO typically presents with a red retina with widespread haemorrhages and a history of sudden visual loss.

- **Central Retinal Artery Occlusion**

A CRAO fundus is pale due to lack of blood supply secondary to artery occlusion. There is typically a history of sudden visual loss.

- **Foreign Body**

Staining with fluorescein detects corneal disruption consistent with penetration by a foreign body.

- **Optic neuropathy**

Reduced visual acuity, positive relative afferent pupillary defect, altitudinal field defects, impairment of colour vision (dyschromatopsia), pain on eye movement. *NB: The most common cause is demyelination due to multiple sclerosis. Optic neuropathy may lead to optic atrophy (pale optic disc).*

- **Optic atrophy**

Pale optic disc.

Case Example

Case Details

A 60-year-old male presents with a history of reduced visual acuity in the right eye. The cause is central retinal vein occlusion (CRVO). The history is consistent with CRVO with no alarming or other features. The only abnormality on examination is a CRVO fundus. Choose the examinations you would expect from a safe GP in a competent 10-minute consultation.

Consensus opinion

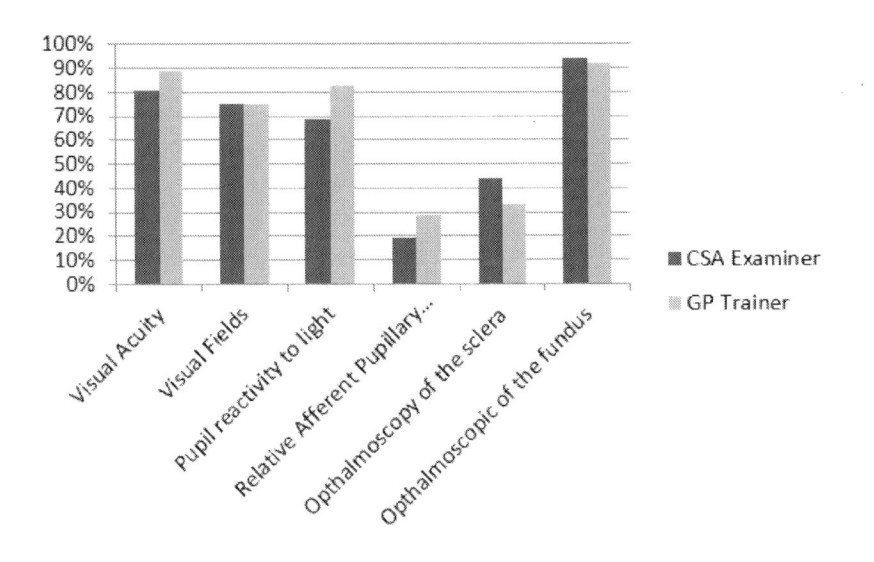

Chart showing percentages for CSA Examiner and GP Trainer across examination components:
- Visual Acuity: ~80% / ~90%
- Visual Fields: ~75% / ~75%
- Pupil reactivity to light: ~70% / ~82%
- Relative Afferent Pupillary...: ~20% / ~28%
- Opthalmoscopy of the sclera: ~45% / ~33%
- Opthalmoscopic of the fundus: ~93% / ~90%

Discussion

In comparison to the red eye case this case focused on the eye prompts examiners to advise different examination components. The difference in the examiners requirements between the eye cases emphasises the importance of correct selection of examination components. The inability to correctly focus your examination will reduce the time available for your clinical management and may negatively impact your data gathering mark. Conversely appropriate selection and performance of the examination components informs the examiner and expert patient as to your capability. The common examination components for cases of visual impairment are visual acuity, visual fields, pupil reactivity and examination of the fundus.

Cranial Nerves

Introducing a Cranial Nerve Examination

An example of a typical introduction:

> 'What you have told me suggests I need to examine the nerves which supply your face. I would like to go through that now'

A pause afterwards allows the patient to provide consent or initiate further discussion and helps to ensure the consultation is shared. Shared consulting will contribute to your interpersonal skills mark.

Cranial Nerve 1 - Olfactory

Ask: 'Has your sense of smell changed recently'

Cranial Nerve 2 - Optic

Test each eye in turn.
  Ask: 'If you wear glasses to read or for distance please put them on if you need to.'
- **Near Sight Acuity Test**
  (use a BNF/leaflet as reading material)
'Can you read the first line on this page?'

- **Far Sight Acuity Test**
'What is the lowest line you can read on the wall chart?'

- **Visual fields Test**
  Test the four corners of vision one eye at a time by confrontation (CN2).

Cranial Nerve 2 and 3 - Optic and Oculomotor

Ask: 'I'm going to shine a light into your eyes; please keep looking straight ahead'.

- **Direct and consensual light reflex testing**
  CN2 is the afferent nerve receiving the light signal, and CN3 is the efferent nerve causing muscle constriction.

- **Examine the optic disc**

Cranial Nerve 3,4,6 – Oculomotor, Trochlear, Abducens

Ask: 'I'm going to ask you to follow my finger with your eyes keeping your head still. Please tell me if your vision becomes blurred or double at any time.'

Trace along the direction of action of the orbital muscles starting from a central point.

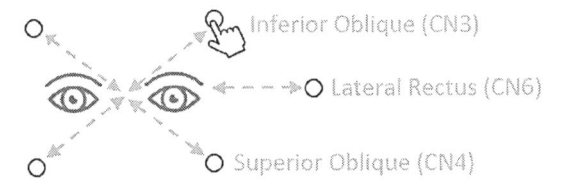

- Inferior Oblique (CN3)
- Lateral Rectus (CN6)
- Superior Oblique (CN4)

Cranial Nerve 5 - Trigeminal

SENSORY COMPONENT
Ask: 'Say yes if you can feel me touching your face. Let me know if it feels different on different parts of your face.'
Touch forehead, cheek and chin. Avoid testing the angle of jaw as this area is not supplied by the trigeminal nerve.

MOTOR COMPONENT
Ask: 'Clench your teeth'
Feel muscle mass at the angle of the jaw.

REFLEX COMPONENT
Corneal reflex is not commonly tested and will not be expected in the CSA.

Cranial Nerve 7 - Facial

Ask: 'Raise your eyebrows.'
Ask: Screw up your eyes and don't let me open them' Attempt to open the eye lids
Ask: 'Blow out your cheeks.'

Look for upper or lower motor neurone involvement.

The upper third of the face receives bilateral innervation from the facial nerve upper motor neurones. Consequently, upper motor neurone damage to the facial nerve leads to palsy of only the lower two thirds of the facial muscles. A facial nerve palsy affecting the forehead is consistent with lower motor neurone damage of which the most common cause is a Bell's Palsy.

Bell's palsy is a case common to general practice and well suited to CSA assessment. In this type of scenario role players will not have physical signs. You may be expected to perform examination following which you will be presented with a card containing your exam findings, or you may be given a card directly after your explanation of the appropriate examination.

Cranial Nerve 8 - Vestibulocochlear

Ask: 'Have you noticed any change in your balance?'
Rub fingers by each ear
Ask: 'Can you hear this?'
If deafness is found on history or examination proceed to the tuning fork tests. Explain each test as you proceed.

TUNING FORK TEST 1: WEBER'S TEST
Ask the patient which ear has reduced hearing. Place the vibrating tuning fork on the centre of the forehead.

Ask: 'Where do you hear the sound?'

Cranial Nerves

Finding	Interpretation
Equal Hearing	No abnormality found. Rinne's test may provide more information.
Louder in the deaf ear	Conductive deafness in the deaf ear
Louder in the good ear	Sensorineural deafness in the deaf ear

Note: Weber's test is the simplest of the two tuning fork tests to interpret and the most informative. If you are clear which ear the deafness is in, interpretation is straightforward.

TUNING FORK TEST 2: RINNE'S TEST
Prime the tuning fork. *Tip: It takes a long time for the sound to diminish in a vigorously vibrating tuning fork. Be time efficient by using a light tap on the elbow or heel of hand to initiate vibration. Tap the arm (tine) of the tuning fork two thirds of the way up from the base.*

Place the **lightly** vibrating fork behind the ear on the mastoid bone.

Ask: 'Tell me when you can no longer hear the sound.'

When the patient reports they can no longer hear the sound move the tuning fork tines in front of and perpendicular to the auditory canal.

Ask: 'Can you hear it now?'

Finding	Interpretation
Air conduction better than bone conduction in the deaf ear	The affected ear is either normal or has mild to moderate sensorineural deafness
Bone conduction better than air conduction in the deaf ear.	The affected ear has moderate to severe conductive deafness **or** complete sensorineural deafness*

Cranial Nerves

*In the case of complete sensorineural deafness in the tested ear, the sound heard is that which is picked up by the healthy ear through bone conduction (a false negative Rinne's test). Rinne's test is less sensitive than Weber's test, needing an air-bone gap of approximately 20dB. Mild conductive deafness may not be detected (a false positive Rinne's test).

The presence of sensorineural unilateral deafness is consistent with acoustic neuroma. Acoustic neuromas form on the cerebellopontine angle which is populated by cranial nerves 5,7,8,9.

Please note that comparison of sound amplitude by alternating the position of the tuning fork between the mastoid position and the auditory canal position is a more subjective test than that suggested here in which the comparison is between the absence and presence of sound.

Cranial Nerve 9 - Glossopharyngeal

Ask: 'Open your mouth and say aah'
Look for deviation of the uvula to one side.
NB: Gag reflex is not commonly tested and will not be expected in the CSA. Cranial nerve 9 is the afferent and cranial nerve 10 the efferent so both are needed for a reflex.

Cranial Nerve 11 - Accessory

Ask: 'Can you shrug your shoulders?'
Test for weakness.

Cranial Nerve 12 - Hypoglossal

Ask: 'Can you stick out your tongue?'
Look for deviation to the weaker side.

Cranial Nerves

Examination Components

The bold text summarises the principle findings in the history

Hearing Loss
Examine CN 8 (Weber's and Rinne's tests, and otoscopy). If unilateral sensorineural hearing loss is found, consider the diagnosis of acoustic neuroma and proceed to examine the remaining cerebellopontine angle nerves 5,7 and 9.

Tunnel vision
Examine CN 2,3,4,6.
Potential causes: Pituitary lesions, Internal carotid artery aneurysm

Visual field defects
Examine CN 2,3,4,6.

Facial pain consistent with trigeminal neuralgia
Examine CN 5.

History findings consistent with raised intracranial pressure
Examine CN 2,3,6.
Look for papilloedema.

Facial weakness consistent with Bell's Palsy
Examine CN 7 and perform otoscopy.
If the whole half of the face is affected consistent with Bell's palsy no further examination may be necessary. If the upper third of the face is spared indicative of an upper motor neurone lesion proceed to examine CN 2,3,4,6,7 for evidence of damage to other upper motor neurones due to central causes such as stroke.

History findings consistent with Facial Herpes Zoster
Examine CN 5,7,8.

Myasthenia Gravis
Examine CN 3,4,6,7.

Cranial Nerves

Examination Clues

- **Acoustic Neuroma**

Unilateral sensorineural deafness +/- impairment of cranial nerve 5 (unilateral loss of sensation), cranial nerve 7 (unilateral weakness of the facial muscles), cranial nerve 9 (uvula deviation).
NB: Acoustic neuroma is associated with Neurofibromatosis Type 2.

- **Pituitary lesion**

Tunnel vision (Bitemporal hemianopia).

- **Raised intracranial pressure**

Papilloedema (blurred disc margins, loss of venous pulsation, flame shaped haemorrhages), third nerve palsy (dilated pupil, with the eye looking down and out) or sixth nerve palsy (loss of lateral gaze). *NB: Expect a history of an underlying cause e.g. intracranial bleeding, tumour, hydrocephalus.*

- **Bell's Palsy**

Unilateral weakness of the facial muscles affecting the whole half of the face (you will recall the forehead has bilateral innervation and is spared in upper motor neurone lesions but affected in lower motor neurone lesions such as Bell's palsy). *NB: Bell's palsy is more common in pregnancy and in diabetes.*

- **Myasthenia Gravis**

Bilateral fatigability of upwards gaze, bilateral ptosis, speech disturbance.

- **Additional**

The following cases can affect any individual cranial nerve.
- Brain Tumour
- Vasculitis
- Diabetes Mellitus
- Multiple Sclerosis
- Sarcoid

Walkthrough Video

Case Example

Case Details

A 39-year-old male presents with unilateral deafness. The cause is acoustic neuroma (AN). There are no alarming features in the history other than onset of unilateral deafness consistent with AN. There are no alarming findings on examination other than unilateral sensorineural deafness consistent with AN. Choose the examinations you would expect from a safe GP in a competent 10-minute consultation.

Consensus opinion

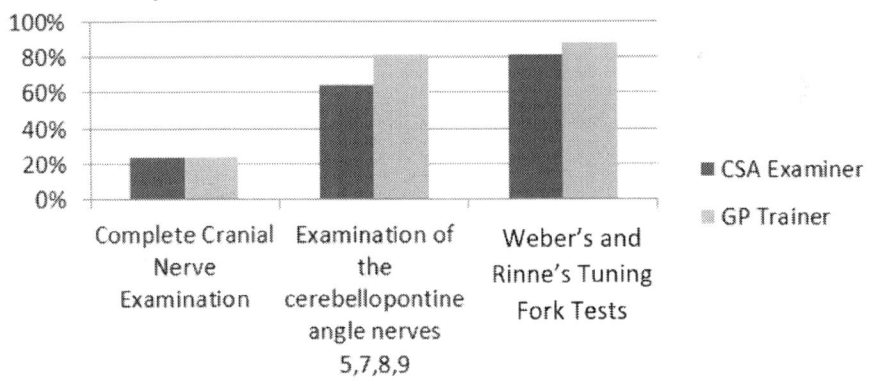

Examination	CSA Examiner	GP Trainer
Complete Cranial Nerve Examination	~20%	~22%
Examination of the cerebellopontine angle nerves 5,7,8,9	~65%	~80%
Weber's and Rinne's Tuning Fork Tests	~82%	~88%

Discussion

The common examination components in this case are a focused examination of the cerebellopontine angle cranial nerves. The message reinforced across the survey is that examination should be focused and selected on the basis of history. A full cranial nerve examination is not required.

Neck

Thyroid Swelling 35
Neck Lumps 37

Thyroid Swelling

Introduction and Preparation

Introduction
An example of a typical introduction: 'What you have told me suggests I need to examine your neck.'

Position and Exposure
Examination of the patient in the chair or standing is common practice. Ensure the neck is fully exposed.

Common Components

Inspection
Inspection findings will not be replicated by CSA role players. If signs are present an examination findings card will be given. The examination card may reveal evidence of thyroid enlargement or asymmetry.

Palpation
Examine from behind. Palpate at rest and during swallowing. Feel for asymmetry and tenderness. Check for lymph nodes (supraclavicular, neck and occipital), pulse rate and rhythm.

Additional Components

History suggestive of hypo/ hyperthyroidism
Examine in more detail for signs of hypo/ hyperthyroidism i.e. proptosis, fine tremor, hair changes, and skin changes of the face and shin.

Case Example

Case Details
A 40-year-old female presents with thyroid swelling. The cause is multinodular goitre. The patient is euthyroid. There are no alarming features in the history. There are no alarming findings on examination.

Thyroid Swelling

Choose the examinations you would expect from a safe GP in a competent 10-minute consultation.

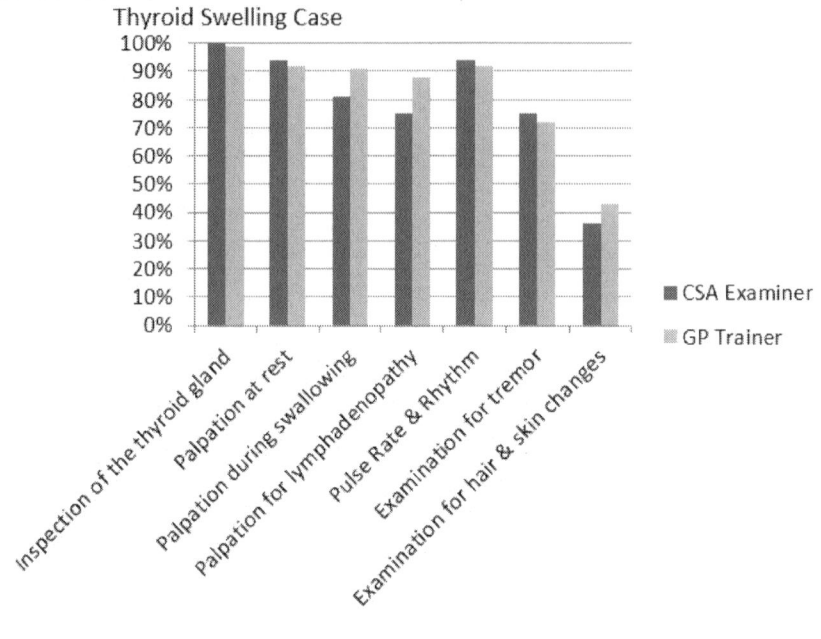

Consensus opinion

Thyroid Swelling Case

[Bar chart comparing CSA Examiner and GP Trainer consensus for examination components: Inspection of the thyroid gland, Palpation at rest, Palpation during swallowing, Palpation for lymphadenopathy, Pulse Rate & Rhythm, Examination for tremor, Examination for hair & skin changes]

Discussion

Common examination components for thyroid swelling are inspection, palpation and focused assessment of thyroid status. Blood tests for thyroid function are routine for those with a newly identified goitre. If present, findings in the examination indicative of thyroid dysfunction can be helpful in explaining the rationale for arranging thyroid function tests.

NICE (CG27) recommends that all new goitres are referred to secondary care. The urgency of referral depends on the examination findings of the goitre. *NB: Most patients with a goitre are euthyroid.*

Neck Lumps

Introduction and Preparation

Introducing A Neck Examination
An example of a typical introduction. 'What you have told me suggests I need to examine your neck'

Position and Exposure
Examination of the patient in the chair or standing is common practice. Ensure the neck is fully exposed.

Common Components

Inspection
Inspection findings will not be replicated by CSA role players. If signs are present an examination findings card will be given. The examination card may reveal evidence of a mass or glandular enlargement.

Palpation
Examine from behind. Palpate the lymph nodes and the anterior and posterior triangles of the neck. Feel for asymmetry and tenderness.

Note: A summary of the management of adult neck masses in primary care advises that most neck lumps present for less than 3 weeks are secondary to infection. In the absence of alarming features in the history or on examination it suggests a strategy of review and onward referral for those with lumps persisting for more than 4 weeks.
 Schwetschenau E, Kelley DJ; The adult neck mass. Am Fam Physician. 2002 Sep 1;66(5):831-8

Additional Components

Submandibular Lumps
Examine mouth for submandibular lumps/salivary gland stones.

Parotid Lumps
Examine the parotid gland and test facial nerve involvement.

Neck Lumps

History suggestive of lung cancer (persistent cough, breathlessness, weight loss)
Examine the respiratory system.

Case Example

Case Details
A 50-year-old man presents with a parotid swelling. The cause is pleomorphic adenoma. There are no alarming features in the history. The findings on examination are typical of pleomorphic adenoma. Choose the examinations you would expect from a safe GP in a competent 10-minute consultation.

Consensus opinion

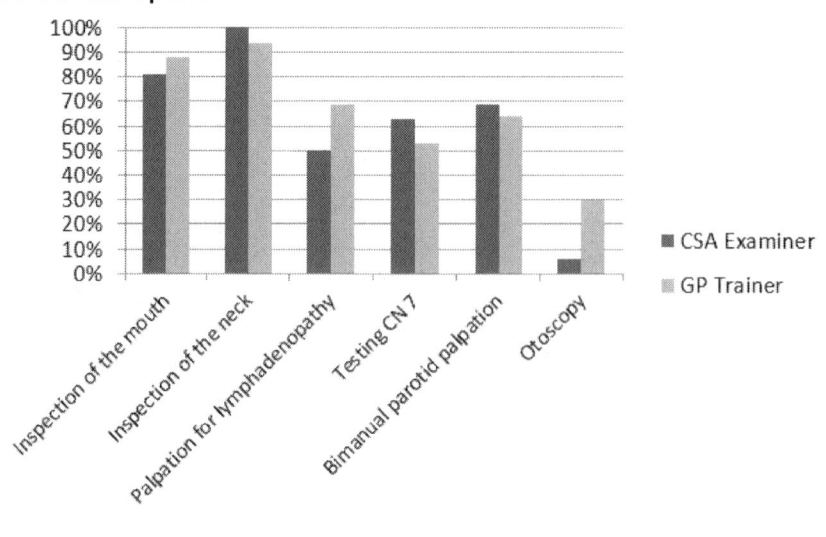

[Bar chart comparing CSA Examiner and GP Trainer responses across: Inspection of the mouth, Inspection of the neck, Palpation for lymphadenopathy, Testing CN 7, Bimanual parotid palpation, Otoscopy]

Discussion
Examiners routinely expect all of the listed components to be commonly examined in patients with parotid swellings excepting otoscopy.

Chest

Breathlessness of unknown aetiology 40

Asthma exacerbation 43

Chest Infection / COPD exacerbation 45

Palpitations 47

Hypertension 49

Breathlessness of unknown aetiology

Introduction and Preparation

Introducing the Examination
An example of a typical introduction: 'What you have told me suggests I should check your pulse, have a listen to your chest, pop a device on your finger to check your oxygen levels and take your blood pressure'. A pause at this point helps to share the consultation by encouraging a response and permitting questions about the examination. Consider offering a chaperone.

Position and Exposure
Examination in the chair or standing is common practice. Expose the back to auscultate the mid and lower zones of the lungs, and anteriorly for the upper zones. Auscultate the heart anteriorly with consideration for patient dignity.

Common Components

Inspection
Inspect for signs of panic, completion of sentences, respiratory rate, use of accessory muscles, pallor, lymphadenopathy/ masses, and elevated jugular venous pressure.
Some of The listed signs here are replicable by CSA role players e.g. breathlessness, others are not. If non-replicable signs are present, an examination findings card will be given.

Palpation
Examine the cervical and axillary lymph nodes.

Auscultation
Listen posteriorly to the chest in mid and lower zones for wheeze, crackles, and breath sounds and anteriorly in the upper zones. Auscultate the heart for murmurs.

Blood Pressure

Breathlessness of unknown aetiology

Pulse & Oxygen Saturation
It is good practice to assess rhythm when assessing rate.

Examination Clues

- **Atrial Fibrillation**

Tachycardia with an irregular pulse.
NB: Consider risk factors in the history e.g. hypertension, lung disease.

- **Anaemia**

Conjunctival pallor.
NB: Consider risk factors in the history e.g. dietary, medication, comorbidity.

- **Aortic Stenosis**

An ejection systolic murmur in the aortic region radiating to the carotids. Left sided heart murmurs are loudest on expiration. Most common in over 65s and affecting up to 10% of patients over age 80.

- **Pulmonary Fibrosis**

Fine crackles in the lungs.

- **COPD**

Hyper-expansion of the chest, increased respiratory effort, wheeze. Most commonly smokers over the age of 35.

- **Heart Failure**

Peripheral oedema, Pleural effusion, Raised jugular venous pressure.

Case Example

Case Details

A 62-year-old man presents with breathlessness. This case is an undifferentiated presentation i.e. the cause is not obvious from the history

Breathlessness of unknown aetiology

given. The patient is a hypertensive smoker with no history of breathlessness or heart disease. The findings on examination are consistent with atrial fibrillation which is not rate controlled. Choose the examinations you would expect from a safe GP in a competent 10-minute consultation.

Consensus opinion

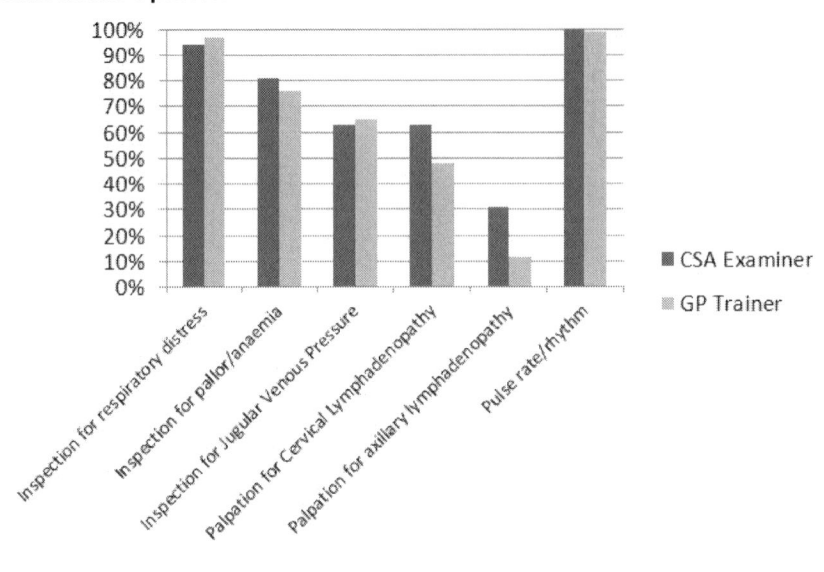

Discussion

The range of examination recommended by examiners in this case is broader than in cases such as the acoustic neuroma presentation where the likely cause is well defined by the history. It is reasonable to draw the conclusion that where uncertainty remains high following history taking a broader approach to examination can be useful to help manage and reduce uncertainty. Be mindful not to slip into a systems approach and where possible use history to guide and focus your examination.

Asthma Exacerbation

Introduction and Preparation

Introducing the Examination
An example of a typical introduction: 'What you have told me suggests I should check your pulse and oxygen levels. I would then like to listen to your chest and measure your peak flow.' A pause at this point helps to share the consultation by encouraging a response and permitting questions about the examination. Consider offering a chaperone.

Position and Exposure
Examination in the chair is common practice. Expose the back to auscultate the mid and lower zones of the lungs, and anteriorly for the upper zones. Peak flow testing should be performed standing.

Common Components

Inspection
Some of the listed signs here are replicable by CSA role players e.g. breathlessness, others are not. If non-replicable signs are present an examination findings card will be given. Look for signs of panic, completion of sentences, respiratory rate, and use of accessory muscles.

Auscultation
Listen posteriorly to the chest in the mid/lower zones for wheeze, crackles, and breath sounds and anteriorly in the upper zones.

Peak Flow
Record the best of 3 blows with the patient standing.

Pulse & Oxygen Saturation
It is good practice to assess rhythm when assessing rate. Chest infections can trigger atrial fibrillation.

Asthma Exacerbation

Case Example

Case Details
A 17-year-old female known asthmatic presents with breathlessness. The cause is an asthma exacerbation of moderate severity. The findings on examination are consistent with an exacerbation of moderate severity. Choose the examinations you would expect from a safe GP in a competent 10-minute consultation.

Consensus opinion

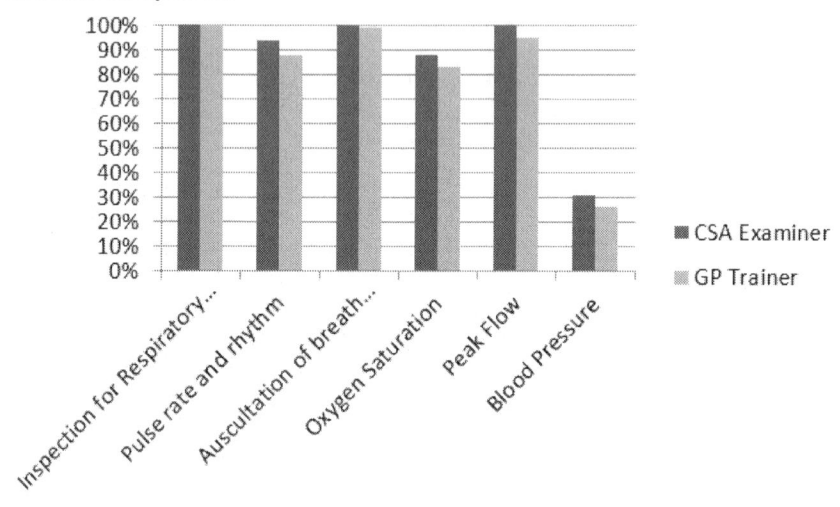

Discussion
In some cases, the choice of which examinations to perform is simplified by the presence of well-defined guidance. In such cases there is a high degree of consensus between examiners and trainers as to the selection of examination components. Asthma exacerbation is one such area.

Chest Infection / COPD Exacerbation

Introduction and Preparation

Introducing the Examination
An example of a typical introduction: 'What you have told me suggests I should check your pulse and oxygen levels. I would then like to listen to your chest.' A pause at this point helps to share the consultation by encouraging a response and permitting questions about the examination. Consider offering a chaperone.

Position and Exposure
Examination in the chair is common practice. Expose the back to auscultate the mid and lower zones of the lungs, and anteriorly for the upper zones.

Common Components

Inspection
Some of the listed signs here are replicable by CSA role players e.g. breathlessness, others are not. If non-replicable signs are present an examination findings card will be given. Look for signs of panic, completion of sentences, respiratory rate, and use of accessory muscles.

Auscultation
Listen posteriorly to the chest in the mid/lower zones for wheeze, crackles, and breath sounds and anteriorly in the upper zones.

Pulse & Oxygen Saturation
It is good practice to assess rhythm when assessing rate. Chest infections can trigger atrial fibrillation.

Chest Infection / COPD Exacerbation

Additional Components

Features of a Severe Exacerbation Present in the History

Blood pressure (used to calculate the CURB 65* score)

* CURB 65 stands for Confusion, Urea >7, Respiratory Rate > 30/min, Blood pressure <90 systolic, age over 65. Each feature scores 1 and a score >2 warrants admission. Regardless of whether a urea result is available the score can be used to help guide your management. An assessment of confusion should be made in the history.

Palpitations

Introduction and Preparation

Introducing the Examination
An example of a typical introduction: "What you have told me suggests I should check your pulse, have a listen to your chest and take your blood pressure. A pause at this point helps to share the consultation by encouraging a response and permitting questions about the examination. Consider offering a chaperone.

Position and Exposure
Examination in the chair is common practice. Expose the back to auscultate the mid and lower zones of the lungs, and anteriorly for the upper zones. With care for patient dignity, auscultate the heart anteriorly.

Common Components

Inspection
Where the history is consistent with thyroid disease inspect for palmar erythema, fine tremor, exophthalmos, evidence of weight loss, and goitre.

Peripheral Pulse
Check rate and rhythm.

Blood Pressure

Auscultation
Listen for murmurs.

In House ECG
ECG is useful as a baseline even if normal.

Palpitations

Examination Clues

- **Atrial Fibrillation**

Tachycardia with an irregular pulse. Murmurs or a history consistent with mitral valve disease. *NB: Consider risk factors in the history e.g. hypertension, lung disease.*

- **Hyperthyroidism**

Tachycardia (sinus or atrial fibrillation), palmar erythema, fine tremor, exophthalmos, evidence of weight loss, goitre.

Hypertension (Newly diagnosed)

Introduction and Preparation

Introducing the Examination
An example of a typical introduction: 'As your blood pressure is raised, I'd like to check a few things to see if there is any effect on your eyes, heart or kidneys. This involves having a look in your eyes, checking your pulse, testing a urine sample for protein, and having a listen to your heart. Is that okay?' A pause at this point helps to share the consultation by encouraging a response and permitting questions about the examination. Consider offering a chaperone.

Position and Exposure
Examination in the chair is common practice. With care for patient dignity, auscultate the heart anteriorly.

Common Components

Blood Pressure
Check blood pressure in both arms*.

Peripheral Pulse
Feel for rate and rhythm.

Urinalysis
Test urine sample for albumin/protein.

Fundoscopy
Examine the retina for evidence of end organ damage.

Palpation
Feel the cardiac apex and chest for thrills.

Auscultation
Listen for murmurs.

Hypertension (Newly diagnosed)

*Guidelines advise blood pressure measurement in both arms. If a difference of >15 mmHg is present, repeat the measurements. If the difference remains, measure subsequent blood pressures in the arm with the higher reading [NICE NG136]. An inter-arm difference of > 15mmHg is an independent risk factor for vascular disease and mortality.

If the blood pressure is raised on the first reading, take a further measurement in the arm with the higher reading. If a decline in blood pressure is found on the subsequent reading, take a third. Record the lowest of the three readings.

Christopher E Clark, Rod S Taylor, John L Campbell. The difference in blood pressure readings between arms and survival: primary care cohort study. BMJ, 2012; 344 DOI: 10.1136/bmj.e1327

Case Example

Case Details

An asymptomatic 49-year-old female presents with high blood pressure readings from her gym. She has no history of note. This is a case of newly diagnosed hypertension (BP 162/94). There are no alarming features in the history or on examination. Choose the examinations you would expect from a safe GP in a competent 10-minute consultation.

Discussion

There are several common components examiners expect you to perform when assessing a newly diagnosed hypertensive patient and a lot to discuss in the management section. To avoid running out of time it helps to be able to know the examination routine off by heart, so you can move through the examination swiftly. Aim to complete the examination section in under 2 minutes. Timely completion of the examination is helped by the fact that you are most unlikely to be asked to perform fundoscopy, urinalysis or record blood pressure. Instead information about these components will be given on an examination findings card.

Hypertension (Newly diagnosed)

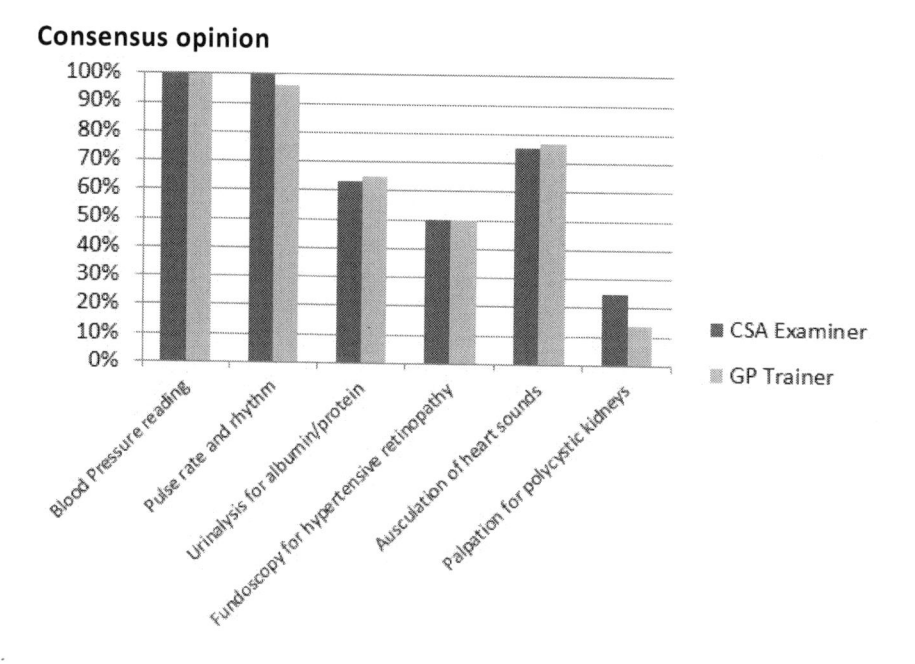

Consensus opinion

Arm

Shoulder 53
Arm neurological 57
Elbow 62
Hand 64

Shoulder

Introduction and Preparation

Introducing the Examination
An example of a typical introduction: 'What you have told me suggests I need to examine your shoulder. Please can you take your top layers off, so that I can see your shoulder clearly.' A pause at this point helps to share the consultation by encouraging a response and permitting questions about the examination.

Position and Exposure
Expose the shoulder. Examination in the standing position is common practice.

Communicating the Examination Effectively
Examination of the shoulder is quickly and clearly communicated to the patient by demonstration of each movement. After each demonstration ask the patient to copy. 'Can you do this?'

Common Components

Inspection
The listed signs here are not replicated by CSA role players. If signs are present an examination findings card will be given. Inspect from front and back with the patient's arms resting by their side looking for bony deformity, asymmetry and muscle wasting.

Palpation
Feel the joint to identify a hot joint, sites of tenderness, and effusion.

Manoeuvres
Test range of movement.

Range of movement
Compare movements on either side.

Abduction
- look for a painful arc between 90-120 degrees

Shoulder

Adduction

Flexion and Extension

Internal rotation
- ask the patient to place their hand on their lower back and move it upwards as high as they can.

External rotation
- particularly restricted in adhesive capsulitis (frozen shoulder). If reduced examine the range of passive movement.

Additional Components

History suggestive of shoulder dislocation or trauma
Apprehension Test

History suggesting impingement or presence of a painful arc
Impingement tests. (Abduction in supination or Hawkins Kennedy test)

Note: There are many different shoulder tests. One reference lists 129. You do not need to be aware of endless variations. For the CSA, it is enough to know the tests listed here which are demonstrated in the video link.

Examination Clues

- **Adhesive capsulitis**
Restriction of all movements, especially external rotation.
NB: Most common in the over 40s and more common in patients with diabetes and thyroid disease.

- **Subacromial Impingement**
A positive impingement test, the presence of a painful arc, moderate restriction of active movements, an improved range of passive movement. Impingement commonly affects patients aged over 35.

Shoulder

- **Rotator Cuff Tear**

Pain and restriction of active movements. Occurs in young and old alike but in the young a history of trauma is common.

Walkthrough Video

Case Example

Case Details

A 64-year-old female presents with shoulder pain and restricted shoulder movements. The cause is adhesive capsulitis. There are no alarming features in the history or on examination. Choose the examinations you would expect from a safe GP in a competent 10-minute consultation.

Discussion

Examiners highlight the importance of exposing the shoulder joint. 100% of examiners surveyed found failure to expose the joint to be unacceptable. Shoulder cases like this are typical of the type of physical examination you will have to perform in the CSA. They are quite doable in the time available, and simple for role players to demonstrate. Think about the scenarios you might see e.g. impingement, shoulder instability, frozen shoulder, rotator cuff tendinitis. Be guided by the history and examination clues. A well-structured, confidently performed, and appropriately focused exam will set you well on the road for a clear pass in shoulder stations.

Shoulder

Consensus opinion

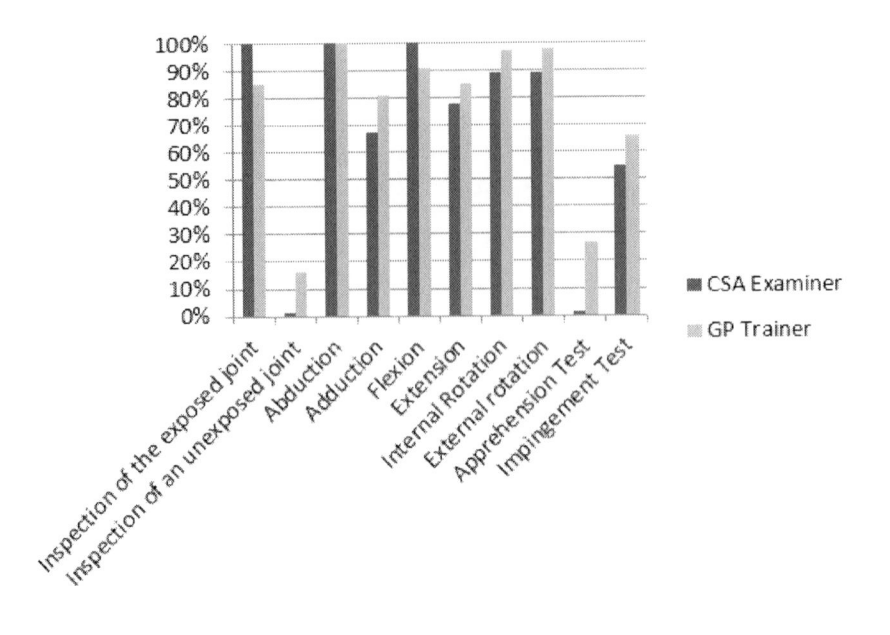

Arm Neurological

Introduction and Preparation

Introducing the Examination
An example of a typical introduction: 'What you have told me suggests I need to examine your arms. Can you take your top layers off, so I can see both your arms all the way up to your shoulders?' A pause at this point helps to share the consultation by encouraging a response and permitting questions about the examination.

Position and Exposure
Expose the arms up to shoulder height. Examination in the chair is common practice.

Common Components

Inspection
Look for asymmetry, wasting, tremor, fasciculation, and lymphadenopathy.

Tone
Feel for cogwheeling and rigidity.

Power

Nerve	Action Tested	Diagram	Instructions
C5	Shoulder Abduction		Hold your arms like this and don't let me press them down
C6	Elbow Flexion		Hold your arms like this and don't let me pull them out
C7	Elbow Extension		Now don't let me push them in
C8	Grip		Squeeze my two fingers as tight as you can
T1/Ulnar	Finger Abduction		Spread your fingers wide like this. Don't let me push them together.

Arm Neurological

Nerve	Action Tested	Diagram	Instructions
Median	Pinch Grip		Make a pinch like this. Don't let me break it

Reflexes
Test supinator (C5,6), biceps (C5,6) and triceps (C7).

Sensation
An example of a typical introduction to sensory testing: 'Please close your eyes and let me know when you can feel me touching your arm. Let me know if anywhere I touch you feels different.'
Touch once in the dermatomes C4,5,6,7,8 & T1,2. Keep the timing of touches unpredictable to help prevent guesswork by the patient.

Figure: Anterior Aspect of the Left Arm

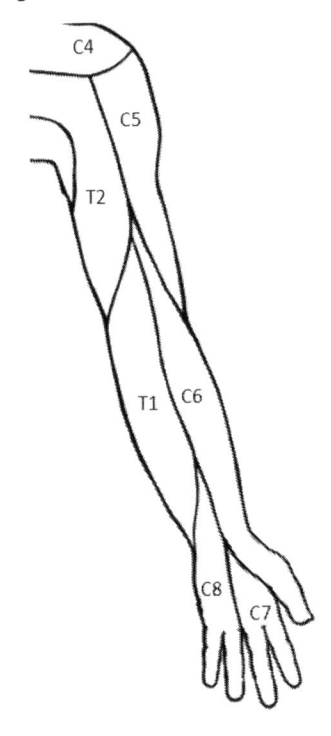

Arm Neurological

Additional Components

History or examination findings suggestive of sensory loss or conditions associated with dorsal column disease
Test proprioception and vibration sense.

History of clumsiness, stroke or evidence of incoordination
Test coordination (finger nose pointing & dysdiadochokinesis).

History or examination of recurrent hand injuries suggesting loss of temperature sensation
Test temperature Sensation (syringomyelia).

Examination Clues

- **Cervical disc protrusion**

Radiculopathy causing reduced range of neck movement with increased pain on neck extension or rotation. Upper limb weakness, paraesthesia, sensory impairment in the distribution of the affected nerve, hyperreflexia in the affected nerve i.e. hyperreflexia of biceps if C5/6 affected, hyperreflexia of triceps if C7 involved.

- **Motor neurone disease**

Presence of mixed upper and lower motor neurone signs i.e. brisk reflexes in a limb with muscle wasting and fasciculation. Signs are mainly motor but sensory signs may coexist. Most common in the 40-60-year-old age range.

- **TIA/CVA**

Upper motor and sensory neuronal signs.

- **Syringomyelia**

Pain, temperature and sensory loss in the arms, shoulders and upper chest. Typically presents in the 20s and 30s.

- **Brachial plexus injury**

C5-T1 motor weakness and sensory loss, often in the context of a trauma.

Arm Neurological

- **Tendon injury - biceps**

A ball-like appearance of the upper arm biceps region. The muscular ball results from the untethered biceps retracting proximally.

- **Polymyalgia Rheumatica**

Bilateral shoulder girdle aching in the over 50s. Stiffness limits the range of movement, but power is retained.

Walkthrough Video

Case Example

Case Details

A 57-year-old male presents with unilateral arm weakness. The cause is a cervical radiculopathy. The history and examination are consistent with cervical radiculopathy. Choose the examinations you would expect from a safe GP in a competent 10-minute consultation.

Discussion

This is a more complex type of case because the number of examination components are greater than in other cases, and the selection, application and interpretation of them requires a good understanding of some relatively complex pathologies. You can simplify the task for yourself by learning the examination steps, so they become automatic. Doing so frees you to concentrate on interpreting the information found during examination. It is readily apparent whether candidates are confident in this type of examination.

Arm Neurological

Consensus opinion

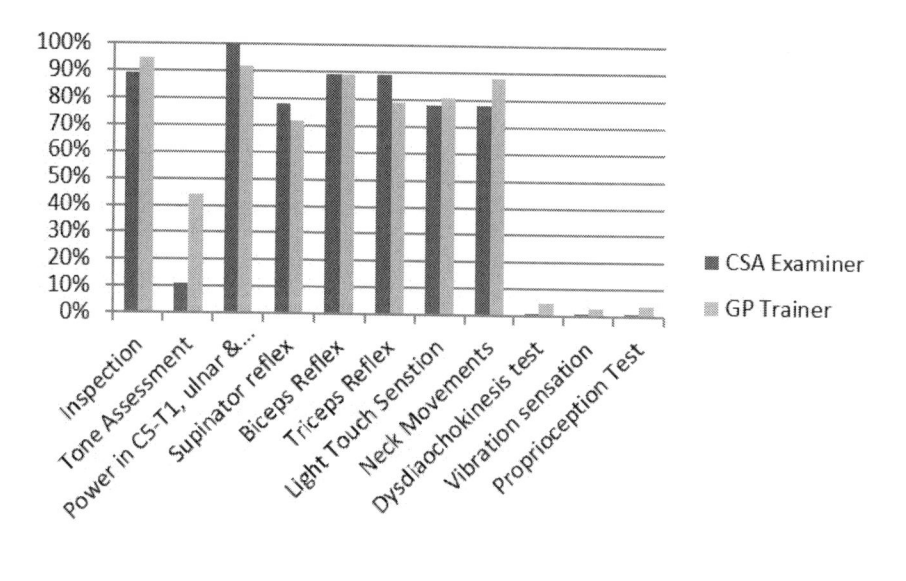

Elbow

Introduction and Preparation

Introducing the Examination
An example of a typical introduction: 'What you have told me suggests I need to examine your elbow. Can you adjust your top so I can see your upper arm and elbow?' A pause at this point helps to share the consultation by encouraging a response and permitting questions about the examination.

Position and Exposure
Expose the elbow. Examination in the chair is common practice.

Common Components

Inspection
The listed signs here are not replicated by CSA role players. If signs are present an examination findings card will be given. Ensure the elbow is fully exposed. Inspect for swelling, redness, scars and deformity, and for the posterior swelling of olecranon bursitis.

Palpation
Palpate for warmth and with the elbow flexed to 90 degrees, palpate the radial head and joint line up to the olecranon.
Palpate over the lateral epicondyle and distally along the common extensor tendon feeling for the localised tenderness of tennis elbow. For Golfer's elbow, palpate over the medial epicondyle instead.

Movement
Demonstrate flexion and extension. Compare the range of movement and check passive movement if active flexion or extension is reduced.
Assess pronation and supination while feeling for crepitus.

Additional Components

History suggestive of lateral epicondylitis (Tennis elbow)
Cozen's Test: with the elbow at 90 degrees and forearm resting palm down on the table, stabilise the elbow with one hand. Ask the patient to make a fist, and with the wrist pronated and radially deviated ask the patient to push up against your hand. A positive test is pain over the lateral epicondyle.

History suggestive of medial epicondylitis (Golfer's elbow)
With the elbow at 90 degrees flexion and rested palm up on the table, ask the patient to make a fist and push up against your hand. Pain is usually felt around the medial epicondyle in Golfer's elbow.

Hand

Introduction and Preparation

Introducing the Examination
An example of a typical introduction: 'What you have told me suggests I need to examine your hand. Can you adjust your sleeve so I can see your hand and forearm clearly?'

Position and Exposure
Expose the hand and forearm. Examination in the chair is expected.

Common Components

Inspection
The listed signs here are not replicated by CSA role players. If signs are present an examination findings card will be given. Expose the forearms, inspect anterior and posterior aspects for deformity and swelling e.g. wrist drop of radial nerve palsy, tremor of Parkinsonism, muscle wasting.

Palpation
Palpate for swellings, joint tenderness, joint temperature, synovitis.

Additional Components

History of Carpal Tunnel Syndrome
Perform Tinel's and modified Phalen's tests (see walkthrough video link). Examine the median nerve, testing power and sensation.

History of Tenosynovitis
Perform Finkelstein's test (see page 66)

History of hand weakness
Examine power in the hand and if positive proceed to the arm neurological examination.

History of Triggering
Palpate the flexor tendons for a trigger nodule.

Special Tests

Tinel's Test
Percuss over the palm towards the wrist to elicit tingling/pain which is more marked in the affected hand.

Modified Phalen's Test
Press over the flexor retinaculum whilst palmar flexing the hand. Exacerbation of symptoms (tingling/pain) is a positive result.

Finkelstein's Test
Ask the patient to hold their thumb in a fist and flex the wrist to stretch abductor pollicis longus.

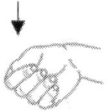

Examination Clues

- **Carpal Tunnel Syndrome**

Sensory loss in a median nerve distribution, positive Tinel's test, positive modified Phalen's test.

- **Tenosynovitis**

Tenderness over the anatomical snuff box. A positive Finkelstein's test.

- **Dupuytren's Contracture**

Thickening of the palmar fascia over a flexor tendon with a fixed flexion deformity.

Hand

- **Gout**

A single, hot, tender joint which may show tophi.

- **Osteoarthritis**

Negative squeeze test, absence of synovitis, presence of bony deformity e.g. Heberden's nodes, Bouchard's nodes.

- **Rheumatoid Arthritis**

Positive squeeze test, hot tender joints, ulnar deviation, swan neck deformity, rheumatoid nodules.

Walkthrough Video

Case Example

Case Details
A 34-year-old female presents with hand discomfort and weakness. She has carpal tunnel syndrome. The history and examination are consistent with carpal tunnel syndrome. Choose the examinations you would expect from a safe GP in a competent 10-minute consultation.

Discussion
Carpal tunnel syndrome and tenosynovitis are cases that lend themselves to examination in the CSA. They are simple for role players to replicate. Both cases are bread and butter to GPs. Consequently, to achieve a pass standard you are expected to perform the examinations fluently and to a high standard.

Hand

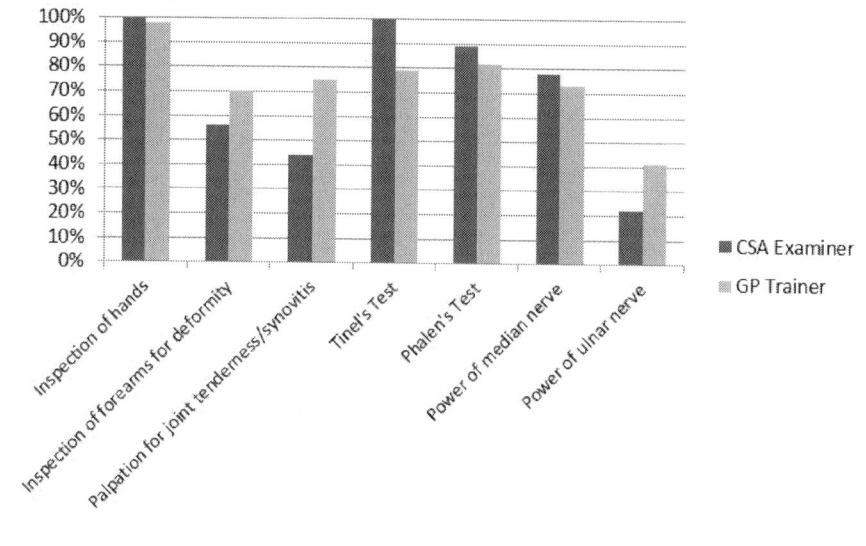

Consensus opinion

Abdomen

Abdominal pain 69
Rectal bleeding 72
Low back pain 73

Abdominal Pain

Introduction and Preparation

Introducing the Examination
An example of a typical introduction: 'What you have told me suggests I need to examine your tummy.' A pause at this point helps to share the consultation by encouraging a response and permitting questions about the examination. Consider offering a chaperone.

Position and Exposure
Expose the abdomen. Examination on the couch is expected.

Common Components

Inspection
The listed signs here are not replicated by CSA role players. If signs are present, an examination findings card will be given. Ensure the abdomen is fully exposed. Inspect the eyes, neck, and abdomen looking for jaundice, pallor and distension.

Palpation
Palpate the neck for lymphadenopathy. After enquiring for sites of tenderness and starting away from these, lightly palpate the abdomen for tenderness and then palpate more deeply for masses. Check common sites of hernias. Palpate the liver, spleen, kidneys, and feel for abdominal aortic aneurysm and lymphadenopathy.

Additional Components

History of cholecystitis
Examine for tenderness of the right upper quadrant on inspiration. On repeating the manoeuvre, the left side is pain free (Murphy's sign).

Abdominal distension present
Percuss for the presence of ascites, as well as the upper and lower borders of the liver.

Abdominal Pain

Urinary tract symptoms
Test the urine (urinalysis).

Abdominal/pelvic pain in a woman of childbearing age
Request a urine sample to test for pregnancy.

History of Gastrointestinal Bleeding
Examine the rectum for evidence of bleeding.

Acutely unwell patient
Measure blood pressure, pulse, and temperature.

Examination Clues

- **Cholecystitis**

Positive Murphy's test for right hypochondrial tenderness.

- **Pyelonephritis**

Unilateral loin and suprapubic tenderness, pyrexia, tachycardia.

- **Diverticulitis**

Abdominal tenderness which may localise to the left iliac fossa, pyrexia, tachycardia.

- **Urinary Tract Obstruction**

Palpable bladder mass and associated tenderness.

Case Example

Case Details
A 37-year-old male teacher presents with abdominal bloating and discomfort. He has irritable bowel syndrome. There are no alarming features in the history or examination both of which are consistent with the diagnosis. Choose the examinations you would expect from a safe GP in a competent 10-minute consultation.

Abdominal Pain

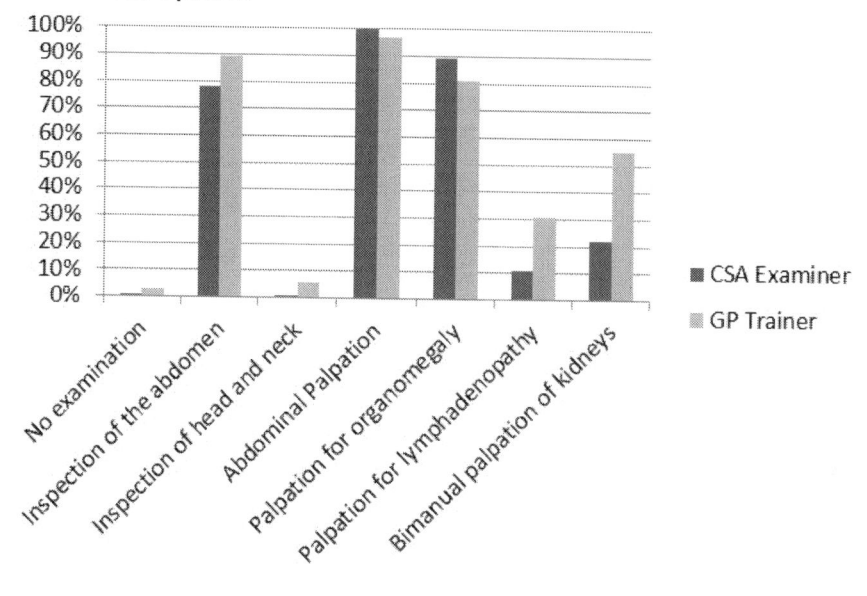

Consensus opinion

[Bar chart comparing CSA Examiner and GP Trainer responses across: No examination, Inspection of the abdomen, Inspection of head and neck, Abdominal Palpation, Palpation for organomegaly, Palpation for lymphadenopathy, Bimanual palpation of kidneys]

Discussion

There are few common components expected by the examiners in abdominal pain cases. Additional components should be applied depending on triggers in the case history or examination. This is another topic easily simulated in the CSA examination - e.g. cholecystitis, appendicitis, gastric ulcer, cystitis, diverticular disease.

Rectal Bleeding

Introduction and Preparation

Introducing the Examination
An example of a typical introduction: 'What you have told me suggests I need to examine both your tummy and back passage. That would involve having a look and feel of your tummy and then looking at the outside of your back passage and using a finger to check inside. Is that ok?' A pause at this point helps to share the consultation by encouraging a response and permitting questions about the examination. Offer a chaperone.

Position and Exposure
Expose the abdomen. Examination on the couch is expected.

Common Components
(You will be stopped before rectal examination and the findings of the examination provided on a card)

Abdominal Examination
As per abdominal examination guidance.

Rectal Examination
- Inspection
- Palpation
- Stool inspection

Examine for external piles, skin changes, fissures, internal piles, masses, and stool appearance. In men, palpate the prostate.

Low Back Pain

Introduction and Preparation

Introducing the Examination
An example of a typical introduction: 'What you have told me suggests I need to examine your lower back. This involves having a look at your back, feeling down your spine for tender areas, and checking for nerve root irritation by testing some leg movements. Is that ok?' A pause at this point helps to share the consultation by encouraging a response and permitting questions about the examination. Consider offering a chaperone.

Position and Exposure
Examine the back whilst standing and check straight leg raise on the couch.

Common Components

Inspection
Inspect the exposed spine from behind looking for deformity or muscle wasting, and form the side looking for the normal lumbar lordosis.
Ask the patient to walk a few steps, turn and walk back, and observe gait. Some signs are replicable by CSA actors, for example gait, others are not. If non-replicable signs are part of the case, an examination findings card will be given.

Palpation
Feel down the lumbar spine for bony tenderness.

Range of Movement
With the patient standing, assess lumbar flexion, extension and lateral flexion.

Straight Leg Raise
Examine for nerve root irritation by testing straight leg raise. The straight leg raise test is approximately 80% sensitive and 40% specific, increasing to 75% specific if the unaffected leg is positive.
J Clin Diagn Res. 2017 May; 11(5): RG01–RG02.
doi: 10.7860/JCDR/2017/24899.9794

Additional Components

'Red flags' of neurological involvement in the history or examination
Perform a full lower limb neurological examination.

Morning stiffness in the history
Inspect for the question mark posture of ankylosing spondylitis.
Observe lumbar flexion & ideally measure distance (Schober's test).

Altered sensation in the history
Test light touch sensation in the thigh, below knee and foot with the leg exposed to thigh level.

Examination Clues

- **Simple low back pain**

Absence of red flags in the history and examination, i.e. no gait abnormality and straight leg raise normal.

- **Cauda Equina**

Presence of lower motor neurone signs in the lower limbs, such as loss of dorsiflexion of the foot and toes with absent ankle jerks. Saddle and perianal sensory numbness.

Low Back Pain

- **Ankylosing Spondylitis**

Schober's test positive for reduced spinal flexion. Question mark posture.

- **Vertebral Collapse**

Bony tenderness at the level of the lesion +/- radiculopathy.

Low Back Pain

Walkthrough Video

Case Example

Case Details
A 39-year-old male presents with 2 weeks of low back pain. The cause is simple musculoskeletal low back pain. There are no alarming features in the history or on examination. Choose the examinations you would expect from a safe GP in a competent 10-minute consultation.

Discussion
For simple low back pain, the assessment can be brief. The CSA examiners indicate the core components are inspection, gait assessment, palpation and straight leg raise testing.

Consensus opinion

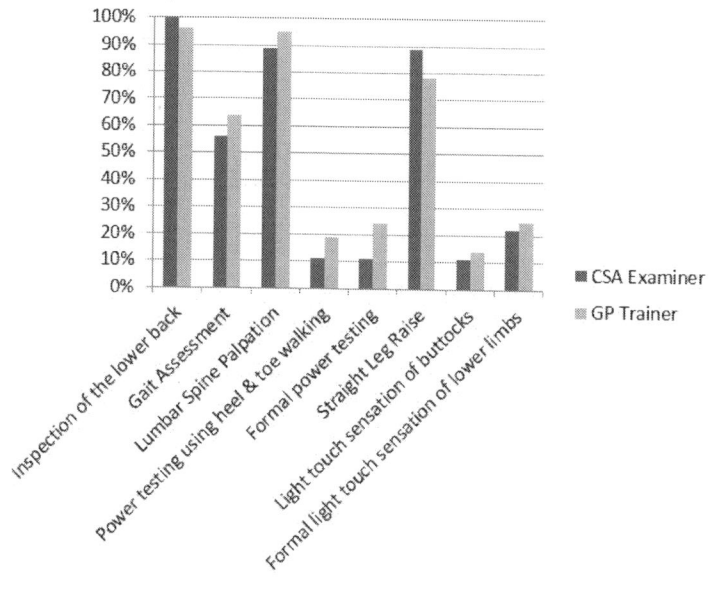

Bar chart comparing CSA Examiner and GP Trainer responses across:
- Inspection of the lower back
- Gait Assessment
- Lumbar Spine Palpation
- Power testing using heel & toe walking
- Formal power testing
- Straight Leg Raise
- Light touch sensation of buttocks
- Formal light touch sensation of lower limbs

Pelvis

Vaginal discharge 77
Pelvic pain 79
Intermenstrual bleeding 81
Male genital 84

Vaginal Discharge

Introduction and Preparation

You will be stopped before pelvic examination, and the findings of the examination will be provided on a card. Nevertheless, you are expected to introduce the examination and the components you wish to examine. Have a low threshold to test for sexually transmitted infections.

Introducing the Examination
An example of a typical introduction: 'What you have told me suggests I need to examine you down below. This involves examining your vagina for any abnormality or tenderness, inserting a speculum and taking swabs. Is that ok?' A pause at this point helps to share the consultation by encouraging a response and permitting questions about the examination. Offer a chaperone. 'For this kind of examination, it is normal to have a chaperone, is that ok?'

Position and Exposure
Examination on the couch is expected.

Common Components

There are no common components in this case scenario. Select the appropriate examination components based on the history.

Additional Components

Bloody discharge post menopause
Inspect for vaginal atrophy and bloody discharge. Perform bimanual palpation looking for masses and insert a speculum to visualise the vagina and cervix. Take swabs for infective causes.

Fishy discharge
Perform a speculum examination and take swabs for infective causes including bacterial vaginosis.

Vaginal Discharge

Non-specific discharge
Perform speculum and bimanual examinations and take swabs for infective causes.

Examination Clues

- **Thrush**

White cottage cheese like discharge, inflammation of the perineum and pruritis.

- **Bacterial Vaginosis**

Thin discharge with a noticeable fishy odour.

- **Sexually Transmitted Infection**

Cervicitis, vaginal or endocervical discharge. Note that examination may be normal.

Pelvic Pain

Introduction and Preparation

You will be stopped before pelvic examination and the findings of the examination will be provided on a card. Nevertheless, you are expected to introduce the examination and components you wish to examine.

Introducing the Examination
An example of a typical introduction: 'What you have told me suggests I need to examine your tummy and down below. This involves examining your vagina for any abnormality or tenderness, inserting a speculum and taking swabs. Is that ok?' A pause at this point helps to share the consultation by encouraging a response and permitting questions about the examination. Offer a chaperone. 'For this kind of examination, it is normal to have a chaperone, is that ok?'

Position and Exposure
Examination on the couch is expected.

Common Components

Abdominal Examination
Examine the abdomen as per the abdominal examination section.

Urinalysis
Test the urine for signs of urinary infection

Additional Components

Woman with childbearing potential
Perform a urine pregnancy test.

Acute pelvic pain or Systemically unwell
Measure blood pressure, pulse rate, and temperature.
Perform a bimanual examination.

Examination Clues

- **Pelvic Inflammatory Disease**

Pelvic tenderness, adnexal tenderness, cervical excitation, mucopurulent discharge, fever.

- **Ectopic Pregnancy**

Woman of childbearing age with pelvic tenderness, cervical motion tenderness, a positive pregnancy test +/- vaginal bleeding.
NB: Typical presentation is between 6-10 weeks gestation.

- **Endometriosis**

Examination usually normal. Haemorrhagic lesions can be present on the cervix or vagina.

Intermenstrual Bleeding

Introduction and Preparation

You will be stopped before pelvic examination and the findings of the examination will be provided on a card. Nevertheless, you are expected to introduce the examination and the components you wish to examine. Have a low threshold for testing for sexually transmitted infections.

Introducing the Examination
An example of a typical introduction: 'What you have told me suggests I need to examine you down below. This involves examining your vagina for any abnormality or tenderness, inserting a speculum and taking swabs. Is that ok?' A pause at this point helps to share the consultation by encouraging a response and permitting questions about the examination. Offer a chaperone. 'For this kind of examination, it is normal to have a chaperone, is that ok?'

Position and Exposure
Examination on the couch is expected.

Common Components

Abdominal Examination
As per the abdominal examination guidance.

Vaginal Examination - Bimanual and Speculum
Look for contact bleeding, cervical excitation, tenderness, discharge, cervical ectropion, cervicitis, ulceration, and polyps.

Swabs
Take high vaginal and cervical swabs for infective causes.

Intermenstrual Bleeding

Additional Components

Woman with childbearing potential
Pregnancy test

Cervical smear due or overdue
Cervical Smear Test

Examination Clues

- **Ectropion**

Redness around the cervical os. Common in teenagers, pregnancy and combined contraceptive pill users.

- **Cervical dysplasia**

Normal cervical appearance +/- red and white patches.

- **Cervicitis**

Mucopurulent discharge, cervical contact bleeding.

- **Fibroids**

An enlarged non tender uterus. A pelvic mass may be palpable abdominally.

Case Example

Case Details
A 40-year-old female presents with Intermenstrual bleeding. The cause is Chlamydia infection and the history is consistent with this. There are no alarming features in the history or on examination. Choose the examinations you would expect from a safe GP in a competent 10-minute consultation.

Intermenstrual Bleeding

Consensus opinion

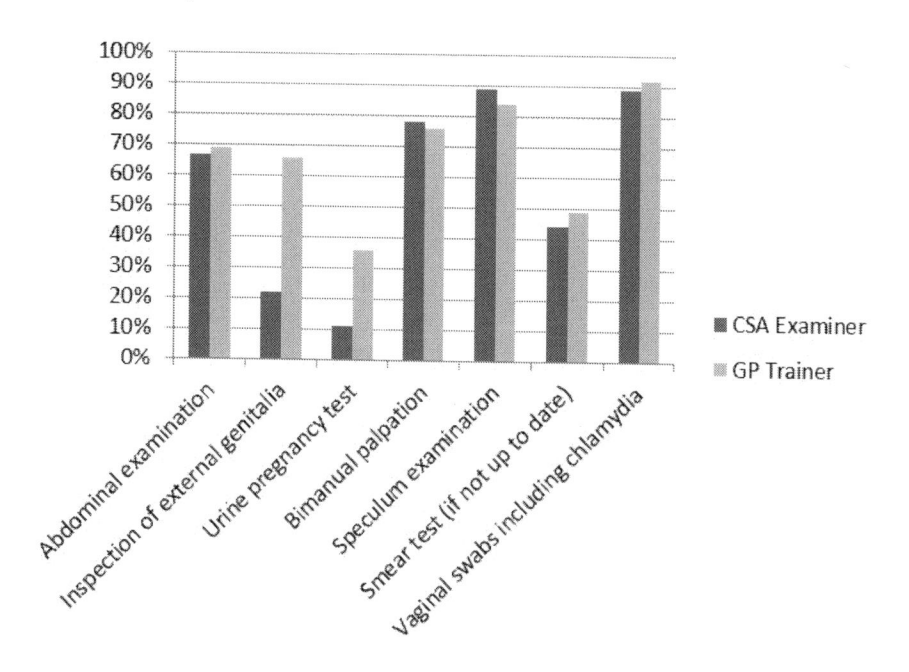

Bar chart comparing CSA Examiner vs GP Trainer percentages for: Abdominal examination, Inspection of external genitalia, Urine pregnancy test, Bimanual palpation, Speculum examination, Smear test (if not up to date), Vaginal swabs including chlamydia.

Discussion

There are some discrepancies here between the examiners and trainers over what should be done. The two affected components are pregnancy testing and external genitalia inspection. This may be because there is limited information in the scenario to inform the decisions to examine these components. Note in both cases the examiners bias is to a focused exam.

Male Genital

Introduction and Preparation

Introducing the Examination
An example of a typical introduction: 'What you have told me suggests I need to examine you down below. This involves checking your abdomen, testicles and penis.' A pause at this point helps to share the consultation by encouraging a response and permitting questions about the examination. Offer a chaperone. 'For this kind of examination, it is normal to have a chaperone, is that ok?'

Position and Exposure
Examination on the couch is expected.

Common Components

Inspection
Inspect the abdomen, testicles, penis glans and shaft looking for ulcers, lumps, and rashes.

Palpation
Feel for lymphadenopathy, plaques, lumps, and areas of tenderness.

Additional Components

Perineal pain or Pain on Sitting
Examine the prostate for signs of prostatitis.

History of epididymal tenderness suggestive of epididymitis
Perform urinalysis and arrange a mid-stream urine sample. Consider testing for sexually transmitted infections.

Testicular masses
Examine the abdomen and inguinal region.

Urethral discharge or painful urination
Consider testing for sexually transmitted infections

Examination Clues

- **Prostatitis**

Tender prostate +/- urethral discharge, fever and inguinal lymphadenopathy.

- **Varicocele**

Scrotal 'bag of worms' present with the patient standing.
NB: 80-90% affect the left side.

- **Hydrocele**

A non-tender, smooth scrotal swelling separate from the testis. The testis may be difficult to palpate if the hydrocele is large.

- **Torsion**

A tender, retracted and swollen testis. Absence of the cremasteric reflex.

- **Sexually transmitted infections e.g. Chlamydia**

Testicular/epididymal tenderness, urethral discharge.

Leg

Hip pain 87
Knee pain 90
Leg neurological 94
Painful foot 96
Peripheral vascular disease and diabetic foot 98

Hip Pain

Introduction and Preparation

Introducing the Examination
An example of a typical introduction: 'What you have told me suggests I need to examine your hip. Is that ok?' A pause at this point helps to share the consultation by encouraging a response and permitting questions about the examination.

Position and Exposure
Examination on the couch is expected. Whilst in some cases it may be necessary to expose the hip to look for abnormalities (e.g. muscle wasting, fasciculation), it is otherwise reasonable to examine the hip without exposing the joint.

Common Components

Inspection
Inspect gait looking for an antalgic limp, a Trendelenburg gait, and a drop shoulder gait (caused by leg length discrepancy).
NB: Trendelenburg gait can result from any cause of painful hip, or abductor weakness. See the walkthrough video demonstrations.

Palpation
Palpate over the greater trochanter for the tenderness of bursitis.
Feel the hip joint for the groin tenderness of arthritis.

Range of movement
Compare movements on either side

Flexion - With the knee flexed at 90 degrees, assess hip flexion. Expect flexion of 135 degrees.

Internal and external rotation – Test rotation with both the hip and knee flexed at 90 degrees. Expect 45 degrees of internal and external rotation.

Abduction and Adduction

Hip Pain

Additional Components

Drop shoulder gait
Assess leg length by squaring off the pelvis and comparing malleoli positioning in the supine position. If a discrepancy is apparent, you can measure each leg length from the anterior superior iliac spine to the medial malleolus on the same side.

Trendelenburg gait
If a Trendelenburg gait is noted during inspection, ask the patient to stand on each leg in turn while observing the level of the pelvis (Trendelenburg's test). When standing on one leg, the pelvis should remain level or even rise on the contralateral side, maintained by the strength of hip abductors in the standing leg. In a positive Trendelenburg's test, when standing on the affected leg, the pelvis drops to the contralateral side due to hip abductor weakness in the standing leg.

History consistent with arthritis
Thomas' test is used to detect fixed flexion deformity consistent with hip joint arthritis. Place one hand under the patient's back to ensure there is no lumbar lordosis i.e. the patients back should touch the couch. Fully flex one hip while observing the resting leg. A normal hip extends as the pelvis is tilted allowing the resting leg to stay on the couch. Flexion of the resting leg as the pelvis tilts indicates a fixed flexion deformity in the hip joint of the resting leg.

Walkthrough Video

Hip Pain

Case Example

Case Details

A 70-year-old man presents with a painful hip (groin pain). The cause is osteoarthritis. There are no alarming features in the history. The findings on examination are consistent with hip osteoarthritis. Choose the examinations you would expect from a safe GP in a competent 10-minute consultation.

Consensus opinion

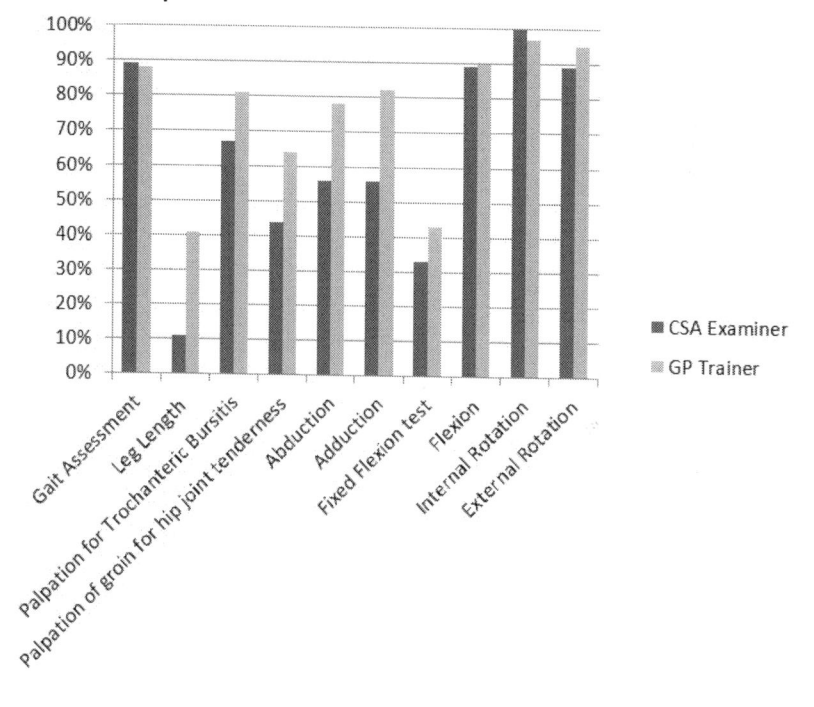

Bar chart comparing CSA Examiner and GP Trainer responses across: Gait Assessment, Leg Length, Palpation for Trochanteric Bursitis, Palpation of groin for hip joint tenderness, Abduction, Adduction, Fixed Flexion test, Flexion, Internal Rotation, External Rotation.

Discussion

Another case that lends itself to examination in the CSA is the hip. This can be time consuming if the patient undresses, particularly if they are frail or disabled. Note that none of the components for hip examination expected by examiners in this case require the joint to be exposed. Whilst in some cases (e.g. groin pain with weakness or sensory changes) it may be necessary to expose the hip to look for abnormalities such as muscle wasting or fasciculation, it is otherwise reasonable to examine the hip without exposing the joint.

Knee Pain

Introduction and Preparation

Introducing A Knee Examination
An example of a typical introduction: 'What you have told me suggests I need to examine your knee. Please could you roll your trousers up or take them off if necessary, so that I can see your knee joints.'

Position and Exposure
Expose the lower limbs from the upper thigh downwards.
Examine range of movement and joint stability on the couch.

Common Components

Inspection
Inspect gait. Inspect the exposed knees whilst the patient is standing, and on the couch looking for deformity, swelling, and effusion.

Palpation
Feel from the quadriceps to the patella tendon for tendonitis. For joint line tenderness and behind the knee for popliteal swelling.

Range of movement
Compare movement on either side.
Test flexion comparing to the normal 135 degrees of flexion (reduced flexion may indicate arthritis or meniscal injury).
Ask the patient to straighten their leg and lift their heel off the couch. Normal extension is zero degrees.

Ligament tests
Collateral ligament tests (with knee at approximately 15 degrees of flexion).
Cruciate stress tests.

Knee Pain

Additional Components

History suggestive of meniscal tear (twisting knee injury)
Please note specific meniscal testing is listed by NICE CKS as a 'do not do' due to low diagnostic accuracy and concern that testing may exacerbate an existing meniscal tear.

Referred pain
Hip examination is indicated if you suspect the knee pain is referred from the hip.

Examination Clues

- **Meniscal Injury**

Knee swelling and effusion, joint line tenderness. The knee may lock or give way.

- **Osteoarthritic knee**

Bony deformity, reduced range of movement, joint line tenderness, stiffness, crepitus, pain on weight bearing, antalgic gait.

- **Anterior cruciate ligament injury**

Positive anterior draw test.
NB: Typically affects younger and more active patients with a mechanism of injury of pivoting through the knee on a planted foot.

- **Collateral ligament injury**

Positive collateral ligament stress test.
NB: A history of lateral impact to the knee or twisting injury is typical.

Knee Pain

Walkthrough Video

Case Example

Case Details
A 48-year-old man presents with knee pain. The cause is a meniscal tear. The history and examination are consistent with a medial meniscal tear. Choose the examinations you would expect from a safe GP in a competent 10-minute consultation.

Consensus opinion

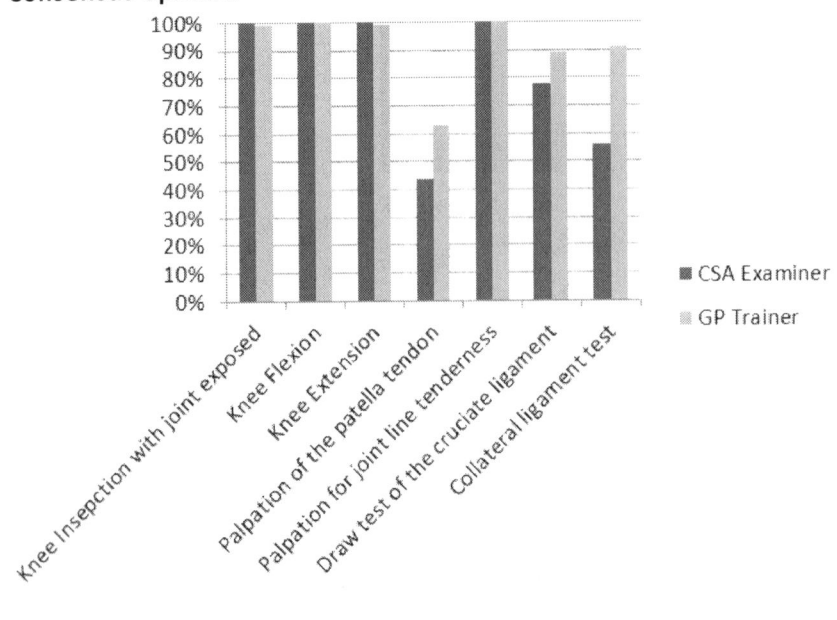

Examination	CSA Examiner	GP Trainer
Knee Inspection with joint exposed	100%	100%
Knee Flexion	100%	100%
Knee Extension	100%	100%
Palpation of the patella tendon	45%	65%
Palpation for joint line tenderness	100%	100%
Draw test of the cruciate ligament	78%	90%
Collateral ligament test	55%	90%

Discussion

If you get a knee case and are familiar with knee examination you should rejoice. You have been gifted an opportunity to score well. Why? Because the number of components that make up the examination is relatively few, little selection of components is required, examination of each component is brief and the interpretation of findings relatively straight forward. Knee problems are common, and hence the topic is commonly examined. We would strongly recommend ensuring you are fluent in knee examination.

Leg Neurological

Introduction and Preparation

Introduction
An example of a typical introduction: 'What you have told me suggests I need to examine your leg. Please can you take your trousers off so I can see your legs clearly?'

Position and Exposure
Expose the lower limbs from the upper thigh downwards and examine on the couch.

Common Components

Inspection
The signs listed here are not replicated by CSA role players. If signs are present an examination findings card will be given. Look for asymmetry, wasting, tremor and fasciculation.

Tone
Examine for rigidity.

Power and Reflexes

Nerve	Action Tested	Instructions
L1,2	Hip flexion	Pull your knee to your tummy
L1,2	Knee flexion	Pull your heel to your bottom
L3,4	Knee extension	Push your heel to the end of the bed
S1	Plantar flexion	Push against my hand
L4,5	Dorsi flexion	Push against my hand

Reflexes
Test ankle (S1,2) and knee (L3,4).

Sensation
An example of a typical introduction to sensory testing:
   'Please close your eyes and let me know when you can feel me touching your leg. Let me know if anywhere I touch you feels different.'

Leg Neurological

Touch once in the dermatomes L1,2,3,4,5, S1. Keep the timing of touches unpredictable to help prevent guesswork by the patient.

Additional Components

History or examination findings reveal sensory loss or conditions associated with dorsal column disease e.g. diabetes, B12 deficiency
Test proprioception and vibration.

Examination Clues

- **Sciatica**

Positive straight leg raise, pain distribution in the buttock which may radiate to the foot.

- **Dorsal Column Disease (B12 deficiency, diabetes)**

Loss of vibration sense and proprioception. Mild reduction in power. In severe cases, an upgoing plantar response and ataxia may be present.

- **Motor neurone disease**

Presence of mixed upper and lower motor neurone signs e.g. brisk reflexes in a limb with muscle wasting and fasciculation. Signs are mainly motor but sensory signs may coexist. Most common in the 40-60 year-old age range.

- **TIA/CVA**

Upper motor neurone signs (increased tone, upgoing plantar response, hyperreflexia) and sensory signs.

Painful Foot

Introduction and Preparation

Introducing a Foot Examination
An example of a typical introduction: 'What you have told me suggests I need to examine your foot. Can you take both shoes and socks off so I can compare your feet?'

Common Components

Inspection
Look for bony deformity, inflammatory changes, corns/blisters, callus, skin changes, nail changes, foot position on standing. Inspect gait.

Palpation For localised tenderness
Ask the patient to identify tender points. The history may suggest a cause, for example the heel pain of plantar fasciitis, metatarsal pain from loss of the transverse arch, pain from an interdigital neuroma (Morton's metatarsalgia) or the hot, red, swollen 1st metatarsophalangeal joint of gout.

Additional Components

History or examination findings reveal sensory loss or conditions associated with dorsal column disease e.g. diabetes, B12 deficiency
Examine the foot pulses and sensation, including vibration and proprioception.

Examination Clues

- **Morton's metatarsalgia**

Pressure on the affected interdigital space compresses the interdigital neuroma and produces pain that radiates to the toe. The third interdigital space is the most commonly affected.

- **Plantar fasciitis**

Tenderness on the plantar surface of the foot localising just distal to the most distal part of the heel fat pad over the insertion of the plantar fascia.

- **Gout**

A hot, red, tender joint, typically affecting the metatarsophalangeal joint of the great toe.

- **Rheumatoid Arthritis**

Positive squeeze test, hot tender joints, lateral deviation, rheumatoid nodules.

Peripheral Vascular Disease and Diabetic foot

Common Components

Inspection
Look for hair loss, skin changes (e.g. hyperpigmentation from haemosiderin deposition), thickening due to lipodermatosclerosis, ulceration, and joint deformity.

Palpation
Check temperature, foot pulses, and capillary refill. If foot pulses are absent palpate popliteal and femoral pulses.

Sensation
Test light touch, ideally using a 10-gram monofilament.

Additional Components

Features of Peripheral Vascular Disease in a patient who hasn't been screened for diabetes.
Dip a urine sample for glucose or use a finger prick blood glucose. A HbA1C or fasting glucose test should be requested.

Moderate to Severe Peripheral Vascular Disease
Ankle Brachial Pressure Index (ABPI)*

*You will not be expected to perform the ABPI in the CSA, however it is a relevant test to request. Ankle Brachial Pressure Index (ABPI) is a comparison of the systolic brachial and calf blood pressure readings. Ratios below 0.9 are associated with vascular disease. Ratios <0.5 are consistent with severe disease.

$$ABPI = \frac{Ankle\ Systolic}{Brachial\ Systolic}$$

Peripheral Vascular Disease and Diabetic foot

Case Example

Case Details
A 64-year-old female diabetic presents with painful pins and needles in her feet. This is a case of diabetic neuropathy. The history is consistent with new onset diabetic neuropathy. There are no alarming findings on examination. Choose the examinations you would expect from a safe GP in a competent 10-minute consultation.

Consensus opinion

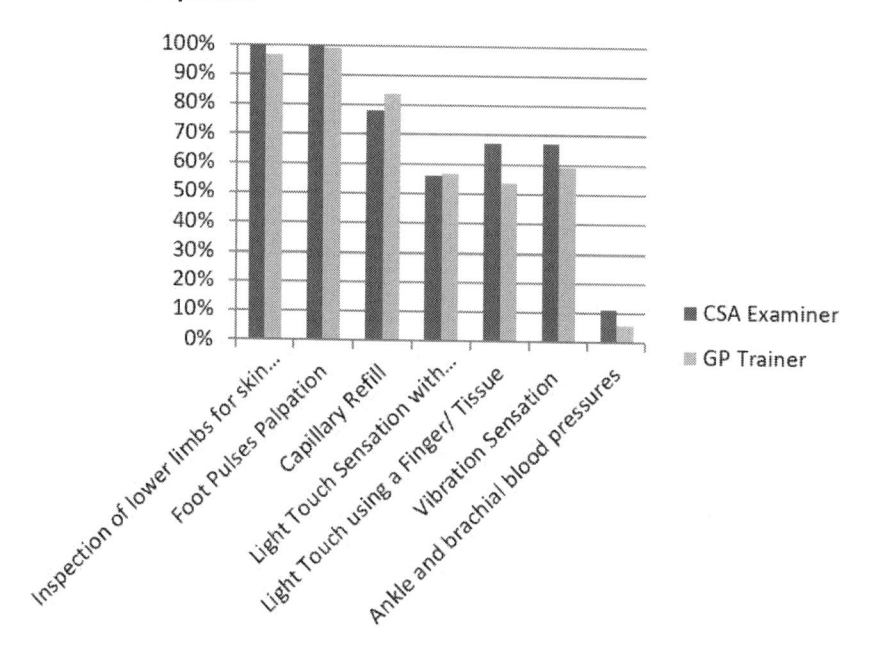

Bar chart comparing CSA Examiner and GP Trainer consensus for: Inspection of lower limbs for skin..., Foot Pulses Palpation, Capillary Refill, Light Touch Sensation with..., Light Touch using a Finger/Tissue, Vibration Sensation, Ankle and brachial blood pressures.

Discussion
The assessment of the diabetic foot is well defined by national guidance hence the high degree of consensus between examiners and trainers. Ankle brachial pressure index measurement is not routinely required.

Printed in Great Britain
by Amazon